"By opening the door to the invisible regions of life—where angels tread—this book, *The Soul of Autism,* turns darkness to light, confusion to insight, and shame to beauty; for, the desperate plight of the autistic is but a metaphor of the "momentous shift," as Stillman terms it, that promises all humanity "a new brotherhood," the ineluctable paradigm shift which erases isolation, neglect, depression, insecurity, dogma and terrible abuse, replacing it all with tolerance, nonviolence, service, knowledge, humility—and love.

> —Susan B. Martinez, PhD, book review editor,
> Academy of Spirituality and Paranormal Studies

"Once again, William Stillman shows us why we must nurture both the intellectual and divine uniqueness of our loved ones with autism."

> —Liane Gentry Skye, author, parent advocate,
> Right to Communicate educational advocate

"*The Soul of Autism* is a balanced and beautiful discussion of what is possible when we look outside our standard world view of those on the autism spectrum. Every parent, grandparent, friend, or educator with exposure to such a uniquely blessed child will relate to the powerful stories of connection and love. In the worlds of the soul, these heart savants may well be our greatest leaders."

> —Robin Rice, creator of Meditationmovie.com
> and author of *A Hundred Ways to Sunday*

"Kudos to the author, William Stillman, for sharing the stories and science in clear, easy-to-read language in *The Soul of Autism.* His respect and integrity in this presentation is outstanding as he shares the stories of intuitive persons labeled autistic and what they can teach us."

> —Caron B. Goode, EdD, coauthor of
> *Help Kids Cope with Stress & Trauma*

D0067049

The
Soul
of Autism

Looking Beyond Labels
to Unveil Spiritual Secrets
of the Heart Savants

By

William Stillman

NEW PAGE BOOKS
A division of The Career Press, Inc.
Franklin Lakes, NJ

THE SOUL OF AUTISM
EDITED BY GINA TALUCCI
TYPESET BY EILEEN DOW MUNSON
Cover design by Ian Shimkoviak/Alian Design
Printed in the U.S.A. by Book-mart Press

To order this title, please call toll-free 1-800-CAREER-1 (NJ and Canada: 201-848-0310) to order using VISA or MasterCard, or for further information on books from Career Press.

The Career Press, Inc., 3 Tice Road, PO Box 687,
Franklin Lakes, NJ 07417
www.careerpress.com
www.newpagebooks.com

Library of Congress Cataloging-in-Publication Data
Stillman, William, 1963–
    The soul of autism : looking beyond labels to unveil spiritual secrets of the heart savants / by William Stillman.
        p. cm.
    Includes bibliographical references and index.
    ISBN 978-1-60163-005-6
    1. Autism—Religious aspects. 2. Spirituality. 3. Autistic children.
    4. Savants (Savant syndrome) I. Title.

 RC553.A88S844 2008
 616.85'882--dc22

                                                    2007046525

For Matthew—

a brilliant point of light

Acknowledgments

Foremost, I praise God for continuing to provide me with blessed encounters, and for loving me unconditionally in spite of my temptations and imperfections.

My gratitude to Frank and Nora for their unwavering wisdom, peerless guidance, and spiritual protection.

My appreciation to Reverend Ziek Paterniti for coining the phrase "heart savant" in homage of Elena, and to my agent, June Clark, for suggesting it be used in the title of this book.

To Nicki Fischer (*www.vibrationregulationtraining.com*), special acknowledgment for her enthusiasm, desire to serve others, and, especially, her passion for involving me in *The Autism Perspective* magazine as well as other ventures.

Loving accolades to filmmaker Teo Zagar for his friendship and creative vision.

Blessings to Gary Zukav and Linda Francis for their mentorship and advisement.

Nancy and Elena of *BeyondtheOrdinary.net* have ardently championed my cause with grace and wonder.

Thanks to Sandie Sedgbeer of *Children of the New Earth* magazine for recognizing an additional forum in which my message may be heard, and for recommending me to New Page Books.

I am privileged by the benevolent support of the following contributors who not only gave their time, but their personal and professional expertise as well:

P.M.H. Atwater, Rhonda Brunett, Rose Bryant, Cherie Castellano, Carla Cappella, Dr. Joe Champion of Interspecies Telepathic Project, Carol Chastain, Renee Chastain, Sabina Childer, Traci Cornette, Cheryl Dejno, Randa Dunmire, Brenda Dunne of Princeton Engineering Anomalies Research, Mary Ann Harrington, Janice Herod, Kim Hewlett, Julia Howerin, Michael Hricko, Michael Jawer, Carol Jones, Macy Jozsef of Living from the Heart (*www.livingfromtheheart.org*), Jesse Kellow, Dr. Kristie Koenig, Theresa Kosinki, Paul Kotler, Sharon McKinney, Penelope McMullen, Genene Murphy, Marty Myers, Marie O'Grady, Paul Parlow, Mary Pritchard, Alisha Raiford-Hall, Dr. Robert Rees of The Institute of HeartMath, Paula Sessing, Kathy Scarfone, Suzanne Shaft, Tammy Shirley, Alex Shutt, Betty Silagyi, Holly Simon, Lois Swope, Gail Venegas, Dr. Jean Weaver, Tricia Weiss, Cindy Wenger (*www.peaceablekingdomac.com*), Birgit Werth, Fred Werth, Debbi West, Karen Williams, and Karly Whalin.

And to the thousands with whom I have had the pleasure of making an acquaintance through consultations, workshops, and presentations, and who provide me with the nourishment to sustain, I thank you most gratefully.

"Mystery surrounds us. It laps at our shores. It permeates the land. Scratch the surface of knowledge and mystery bubbles up like a spring. And occasionally...a tempest of mystery comes rolling in from the sea and overwhelms our efforts..."

—Chet Raymo
Honey from Stone: A Naturalist's Search for God

Contents

Introduction 15

Part III
Higher Ground

Introduction

"**O**kay, here's a weird theory and something to think about: Because our children are sensitive to sights, sounds, smells, and so on, could they possibly be more in tune with the Spirit world as well? Bear with me here. No, I'm not nuts...." So began a late-March 2006 posting to an Internet autism message board from a bewildered but intuitive mother. Her message told of unusual circumstances surrounding her young son's preoccupation with a photograph of his long-deceased great-grandfather—someone who he had never met, but seemed to "know" regardless. The mother related how great-grandpa's picture incites smiles and giggles in her boy (no one else's image causes this reaction); that he'll look up and visually "track air" through the house, and he will wave at someone she can't see, then bid a "bye-bye" farewell. She concluded her message wondering why she hears her son awaken in the middle of the night pealing with playful laughter and then, suddenly saddened, he'll lament "all gone" as the incidents dissipate.

This mother's inquiry sparked great interest, and the message thread received nearly 1,200 hits in just a few days as more moms chimed in—clearly it struck a responsive chord. (A subsequent post on the same topic ran 10 pages and received

more than 3,000 hits!) I wasn't surprised. I had seen—and
sensed—this nascent groundswell for some time, only now it
was gaining momentum. Its timing was serendipitous; my book,
Autism and the God Connection, was simultaneously poised
to be published. It was the first work of its kind to explore the
multisensory spiritual abilities of many highly sensitive people
on the autism spectrum, and contains anecdotes virtually identical to those posted on the autism message board, and the
other postings that followed.

By then, the topic of spirituality was also cropping up in
autism journals. In her article "Kindred Souls," Chris Dodds,
mom to son Taylor, wrote, "I'll never forget the night I heard
him crying in bed and went in to see what was wrong. 'Man
should never have evolved,' he sobbed. 'We're wrecking the
planet and destroying everything that's good about it.'" At the
time, Taylor was just 7 years old. Keri Bowers, whose son
Taylor Cross created the film, *Normal People Scare Me*, penned
her own spiritual epiphany, "One night just after Taylor's first
birthday...I once again asked, 'Why me God?' With my fists
clenched—my mind in victim mode—tears wet my pillow. How
could this happen to me? And then, I heard a big, yet little,
voice saying to me, 'Why not you, Keri? Why not?' At first I
was startled; then a knowing came over me. My time to learn
acceptance had come." Even Ellen Notbohm's respectful and
efficacious *Ten Things Every Child with Autism Wishes You
Knew*, then recently published, addresses kindred musings in
her closing chapter, pondering that her own son *chose her*.

Concurrently, additional parallels emerged. I learned that
the woman who was about to review my book on her radio show

had a son with autism. He informed her that, prior to his birth, he chose her over a Japanese couple. Another radio host called to share her own amazing anecdote: She was caught unaware one day as her young son with Asperger's Syndrome regaled her with nuances about fishing, including knowledge of squid, that, when gently pressed, he revealed was acquired from his great-grandfather, an avid seaman. The thing is, the great-grandfather had died when the woman was 16 years old.

Actress Sigourney Weaver, starring as an autistic in *Snow Cake*, kicked off the film's 2006 Berlin Film Festival premiere with a press conference during which she reflected upon autism through a spiritual prism surprisingly similar to the principles of my work: "I think we have to begin to see it as a gift. We may not understand what it's there for, but if you're in the presence of someone with autism you learn so much. You learn how to play, you learn how to see things, you learn how to experience things, and how jarring the world is." Likewise, actor Joe Mantegna, father of 18-year-old Mia, waxed philosophic about his daughter's autism saying, "I really believe there is a plan out there...it's almost easier to believe in something than not, when you look at all the beauty and wonder in the world...you have to think there is some sort of logic to it, we're evolving toward the light. If this is part of the plan, I accept my role gladly and graciously."

A Spiritual Shift

Similar to many people with Asperger's Syndrome, that most mild of autism spectrum experiences, I have a keen eye for detail, and I tend to reflect upon issues in a global sense, because I'm don't want to filter anything out. And similar to 7-year-old Taylor Dodds, I, too, have agonized over expansive, grand-scale affairs that threaten to affect us all. I began noticing (and carefully stashing away for future reference) a number of indications that our society, as a whole, was open to a spiritual shift in perception—or at least open to discussion and debate about unspoken possibilities, particularly where people with disabilities are concerned. (I now find it intriguing that my hotel soap wrapper extols, "Let the naturally relaxing essence of lavender enhance your mood and calm your *spirit*." I'm not sure that just a few years prior such language would fly.)

Several months before, a *Time* magazine article, "The Down Dilemma," weighed the options for pregnant women arising from the Institute of Child Health and Human Development's new first-trimester screening for "genetic aberrations, including Down [syndrome]." The screening, The First and Second Trimester Evaluation of Risk (FASTER)— with its 96-percent fully integrated detection rate—makes it potentially easier for women to abort their Down-identified fetus far earlier in their pregnancy than before, a choice that 80 to 90 percent select. The flipside is the outcry from seasoned parents who oppose the convenience of terminating the life of a child with a different way of being *because of* his or her way of being. "Will people open their eyes to the possibilities of these kinds of kids?" wondered Patricia Bauer, former *Washington Post* editor and mom to a 21-year-old daughter with Down syndrome—a daughter who, Bauer advocates, is a "source of joy and delight" in her life and that of her family. Could a comparable debate for screening the undesired fetus with autism be far behind?

In June 2006, London's *Daily Mail* reported on the "ethical row" resulting from an improved screening method to create "designer babies." That is, via a sex-selection technique, healthy male embryos could be discarded (as autism is at least four times more prevalent in males), supplanted by female embryos to "dramatically reduce the risk" of genetic autism in families so predisposed. The plans were condemned by Simone Aspis, parliamentary and campaigns worker for the British Council of Disabled People, who advocated, "Screening out autism would breed a fear that anyone who is different in any way will not be accepted. Screening for autism would create a society where only perfection is valued."

The reverberations from the court ruling to terminate Terri Schiavo's life were also still making news. Schiavo, you'll recall, was the woman who, in 1990 at age 26, unexpectedly collapsed in her home, resulting in irreversible brain damage. Physically, she underwent a transformation and became someone who, outwardly, was the most severely impaired and disabled of human beings—unable to speak or move, and totally dependent upon others for her care and well-being. Schiavo's husband contended she was in a persistent vegetative state with no consciousness and no hope of recovery; indeed, Schiavo's postmortem autopsy confirmed as much. (For the record, in March 2007, a Colorado Springs woman named Christa Lilly emerged from an identically described coma after seven years, and the following June, a Polish man recovered after being comatose for 19 years.)

But who are we to define "consciousness"? Aren't human beings hardwired with the will to survive? If not, we'd be careless and apathetic about our own safety, or even suicide. Despite enduring the extremity of her transcendence, and contrary to her husband's adamancy, who's to say that Terri Schiavo *didn't change her mind and choose life*? After appealing to Congress, the Supreme Court, the Vatican, and the White House, Schiavo's parents lost the battle to save their daughter's life, and Terri was allowed to dehydrate and waste away. Her sister publicly decried society's "quality of life mentality" and chastised a culture that has "lost sight of the value [and] sacredness of all human life." There are indeed people who consider individuals with autism, Down syndrome, mental retardation, and other developmental differences, society's "throw aways." In another place and time, the quality of life of such individuals was also deemed unworthy, and they were exterminated en masse.

In an era when the battle lines were being distinctly drawn for opposing sides of the evolution-versus-intelligent design controversy (*Time*'s Nobel-winning physicist, Eric Cornell, condensed it to "The idea that the sky is blue because God wants it to be blue existed before scientists came to understand Rayleigh scattering..."), an unpretentious young man with autism made headlines around the world. Seventeen-year-old Jason McElwain garnered instant acclaim for scoring 20 points in four minutes for his upstate New York high school basketball team, thus propelling them into the season finals. Jason—who didn't start speaking until he was 5 years old—was the team manager who usually sat on the bench; it was his first time playing on the court. News of Jason McElwain's spectacular show quickly spread via the Associated Press, ESPN, and other media sources. His family began fielding a flood of Hollywood movie offers almost immediately, a bobble-head doll was cast in his image, and before long, Jason was partaking of the penultimate American photo-opportunity: posing with President George W. Bush, who admitted "I wept, just like a lot of other people did," when he watched the broadcast of Jason's winning footage.

At the same time the country was lauding this phenomenal accomplishment, another young autistic, Matthew Moran, was also making news, though to a far lesser extent. A letter received by Matthew's Lake Havasu City, Arizona, family from their church informed them that, because the 10-year-old boy with autism could not reliably consume his Communion wafer (Matthew is sensitive to swallowing certain food textures—a challenge for any number of autistics), he cannot partake in the church's most meaningful sacrament because "he is, in fact, only simulating doing so."

The outrage and indignation inspired by this act of omission (not to mention Matthew's personal heartache—he "screamed and cried because he did not get his Communion," reported his mother) led church leaders into a mad scramble of what was characterized as hypocritical finger-pointing. Matthew's father believed the church was violating the *Guidelines for the Celebration of the Sacraments with Persons with Disabilities*, a document of the U.S. Conference of Catholic Bishops, which states that "cases of doubt should be resolved in favor of the right of the baptized person to receive the sacrament. The existence of a disability is not considered in and of itself as disqualifying a person from receiving the Eucharist." This allowance is so obvious that committing it to print seems patronizing. In light of this, Roberto Dell-Oro, Loyola Marymount University theologian—and father of an autistic son—summarized it best when he said, "I'm sure God knows that [Matthew] is receiving Communion."

Contradictory to a published report in *The Catholic Sun* that itemized his parish's rehabilitative efforts, Matthew's full inclusion was never reinstated as insinuated. "It's the only place where he's been bullied that I would think to take him back to," his mother, Jean Weaver, confided with reluctance nine months later. She said the church did acquiesce with a concession: a condition of Matthew's return is that he must occupy the backmost pew distinguished by a plaque that reads, "Reserved for the feeble and infirmed." (The family declined.) I wondered if, at any time in his life, Matthew Moran would ever achieve enough to be afforded the same photo opportunity as Jason McElwain, now dubbed the "autistic hoops fanatic" by the media.

It seems the timing of *Autism and the God Connection*—with its message of reverence, respect, and regard—couldn't have been more fortuitous. I was to be the humble recipient of an affirming shower of outpourings and loving accolades from parents, professionals, and those with autism from around the globe who understood clearly the spirit of my intent. Reading my daily e-mails, I was often reduced to a weepy puddle. A young boy from Florida, inspired by my credo of entitlement for those unable to speak, wrote a touching poem for me. Those who were engrossed by the book told me they couldn't put it down, couldn't sleep, and were reading it a second time because it was "wonderful," "amazing," "powerful," "haunting," and "beautifully written." But the piece de resistance came from the Virginia mom who wrote to tell me that her 2-year-old son "picked your book up off the coffee table and immediately turned the book over to the back cover, pointed to your picture in the lower corner, and took his hand and patted his chest—this is his way of telling us that something is 'his.'" Still others absolved themselves of long-held I-knew-I-wasn't-crazy stories of their own, some of which are included here. Believers were now prepared to give and receive the spiritual truth about autism and other so-called disabilities.

An interviewer asked me if I thought that some of the interest in my book and my ideas may come from the parents' need to find special talents in a child who appears to have few special abilities. The family members who contact me are usually simple, modest people who are often both reticent and relieved to tell their stories. Their language is plain, and I sometimes must edit grammar and misspellings. I elaborated further in my steadfast reply:

> Let's acknowledge that parents of individuals with autism can have intensely complex lives. No one who has contacted me has asked for anything other than the opportunity to be heard, so there's no personal gain involved. And I'm not exploring anything that's not already very well known to countless families; I'm merely illuminating it, bringing an aspect of autism to light that was previously "closeted." So I've not "created" this whole "autism and the God connection" movement, it was already there, unfolding silently but surely. All children are precious and, as human beings, we are all blessed with gifts and talents regardless of who we are.

Measuring Miracles

For those of us not privy to the ease with which others tap their spiritual resources, we may ask, "How does it work?" In pursuing answers, this new book endeavors to build upon and further explore the concepts put forth in *Autism and the God Connection*. You might be wondering how I screened the anecdotes shared in that volume and the one you're now holding. I use two criteria:

1. Is there a ring of truth and an air of humility to what someone is sharing? That is, does the information include nuances credible to the autistic experience without glorifying it unreasonably? In other words, it shouldn't pass muster that those with autism be polarized in the extreme as "God's special angels" because that's not real life; I think it can be an exceptionally challenging lifestyle for any individual on the spectrum as well as her parents and caregivers. That doesn't mean that spiritual giftedness can't manifest, but when it does, it occurs tangentially amidst daily travails of mutual living, learning, and endurance. Most often, people just feel relieved to know that they're not crazy, not alone in the experience, and have found someone who understands.

2. Does the information fall into one or several "themes" I saw emerging as my work progressed? These themes include results occurring from the presumption of intellect and the enactment of the path to opportunity described in *Autism and the*

God Connection, the autistic one fostering spirituality within the family previously indifferent or void, and uncommon attraction to—and innate respect for—nature (plant life, forests, trees) and bodies of water (lakes, streams, ponds). Other prominent themes are:

- *Knowledge of existence before birth*: Telling parents they were "chosen" with deliberate intent; relating information about being in Spirit, or in Heaven, prior to birth; detail about having lived in another time and place (for example "When I was big like you mom…"); fluent in an unrecognizable language, or a language to which the autistic individual has never previously been exposed.

- *Precognition or premonition*: Knowing what was going to occur before it actually did, which may be as simple as accurately predicting next week's school lunch menu, or as urgent as tantruming to avert an unforeseen highway accident.

- *Telepathy*: Exchanging or tapping into thoughts and images with another, usually a loved one such as mom, dad, or grandma, which may include a verbal reply from the autistic person to a mental question not directed to anyone in particular.

- *Animal communication*: Silently intuiting and interpreting "animal speak"—emotions or image-exchange—from domesticated or feral animals. Such interactions may be witnessed by others and deigned extraordinary or unusual.

❁ *Connection with a loved one in Spirit, usually a grandparent*: This may include a strong attachment to the deceased person's photograph, and intimate, previously unknown knowledge about their lives; such conduct may be supported by eyewitnesses and photographic evidence including spheres of energy or "orbs" (as on the cover of this book).

❁ *Apparitions of discarnate, wayward souls or "ghosts"*: For the autistic individual so plagued, this may manifest in extreme, agitated anxiety, night-terrors, and reports of seeing unwelcomed entities, and may be supported by historically verified facts, eyewitnesses, and/or photographic evidence. Families who are particularly religious may refer to such presences as "demons."

❁ *Communion with benign, ethereal entities defined as angels by some*: This may manifest in a two-way interaction in the same place, at the same time, on a regular basis (sometimes daily) from which the individual emerges jubilant and replenished. This may be supported by eyewitnesses and photographic evidence including streaks or bursts of unexplained white light.

To the uninitiated, the preceding may seem unsettling if not unbelievable, but there are those families for whom it is

very real. Still others may attribute such anecdotes to childhood imaginings or psychotic hallucinations. Indeed, on occasion I'll receive a story that begins plausibly enough, but
quickly unravels into what feels like a rambling delusion, the
type that threatens to undermine the credability of my work.
There are those who believe they're communicating telepathi-
cally with an autistic child, but then go on to suggest he's the
second coming of Jesus Christ...he's half-human, half-
alien...he manifests stigmata...he's appointed to world
prominence...should be worshipped and followed en masse,
to give a few examples. Such may be others' reality—just as
each reader is entitled to question or to dismiss some or all of
what I'm presenting—but, for my purposes, I'm listening for
instances of humility amid despair and perseverance.

Contrast the overzealous, grandiose tone of the preceding scenarios with the gentle, unassuming anecdote sent to
me by Holly from Oklahoma, mom to a toddler with autism:

> Our 3-year-old daughter has been having awful, gro-
> tesque nightmares about snakes and spiders. She had
> one the other night about spiders. She screamed out
> once, but that was all. My husband went to get her and
> brought her to bed with us. (I know, terrible habit.) Any-
> way, on his way to her bedroom, he thought he saw some-
> one, and he yelled "Hey!" to scare them. (Last month we
> had a nighttime intruder in our home.) It scared me to
> hear my husband yell like that, but he later told me he
> just felt like someone was there, and he was "making sure."

Well, the next day I was making our daughter's bed, which she had totally destroyed—all the sheets and pillows were on the floor—and I was teasing her about it. She started talking about her bed, and how there were no more spiders in it; how she had talked to "the people in the sky" and that's what the man had said. I said "What? Who?" She replied, "The people in the sky, up there," and she pointed up at her ceiling. I was really intrigued, and kept asking her more questions, but she would only laugh at me and try to change the subject ("Look, mom, I can touch my toes to my nose," and so on). But I found out from her that they were "really big like mommy and daddy"; she cupped her hands and held them high up at her sides, almost like tall wings—although I didn't ask her that. They were "white" and "the man" had "brown hair." She kept saying "people" but only the man had spoken to her and told her there were no more spiders in her bed.

I suppose a lot of people would say it was a 3-year-old's imagination, or another dream of hers. But doesn't it make you wonder? And you think, why would angels bother to tell a little girl there were no spiders in her bed? But then, what is too insignificant to care about?

The Significance of Being

What *is* too insignificant indeed? The answer is, nothing at all. I wouldn't have understood this pragmatism when I first began my spiritual journey as an autism consultant—I'm not sure I understood it even as I was in the midst of composing my book, *Autism and the God Connection*. Coming to this real-ization was a result of wondering on the words already in place, a phrase that awaited my museful mulling.

Autism and the God Connection concludes with an elo-quent soliloquy, profound in its simplicity—so profound that the true intent eluded me until well after the book was writ-ten. In this particular passage, my dear friend Michael, then 15 years old, discusses his perception of being in the world as an autistic, what he defines as a whole soul in a broken body, as opposed to the commonest incarnation—a broken soul in a whole body. In other words, his soul, and others similar to his, emphasizes cerebral over physical, aesthetics versus ma-terialism, spiritual over corporeal. Michael contends that per-ceived disability is not without compensation—aptitude for accessing God at will—lending to its status as a mixed bless-ing. He suggests that "God loves the act of being and what He is depends upon who we are in the physical. When He experi-ences Himself in His highest form the soul returns to the whole. Before that can be possible, God has to evolve in each of us...how all come to benefit God is in bringing Him the sen-sation of being. He gets to see and experience His Godliness through us."

"He gets to see and experience His Godliness through us" was an endearing sentiment, but I failed to grasp the notion in its entirety with purposeful intent. Until one balmy afternoon, as I laid outstretched on my back porch, eyes bleary from read-ing, I gazed out the window at an austere sky punctuated only by an errant cloud. As I watched idly with heavy lids, the cloud swelled as it pulsed before the midday sun, then splintered apart into slow-motion halves like strands of cotton candy. In that moment, I was awestruck: this vision was intended for me and me *alone*. There was no one else in the entire world that had experienced exactly what I just witnessed in that precise moment and from the same exact vantage point. God *was* experiencing His Godliness through me—and only me—in that very instant. If I played this out, God was *constantly* experiencing His Godliness every moment of every day, not only through me, but through *all* humankind, each contributing his or her own unique variation of "being" for God. Imagine the gamut of human emotions and experiences—nothing, no aspect of humanity, escaped being inconceivable, from intense suffering to euphoric elation. And *nothing* was too insignificant.

But there was more. Wasn't God also experiencing Himself as the passing cloud? There would never be another one to divide itself in precisely the same way again. Further still, what about every microscopic mite that tills soil beneath each blade of grass upon which falls individual snowflakes? Or the myriad grains of sand that pebble every beach? Expand this concept to include the entire *universe*, and the possibilities of "beingness" are infinite! Nothing and *no one* was without purpose for being—even, or *especially*, those with different ways of being. Michael's glorious, astute comprehensions now resonated with certain clarity as my cloud silently sifted from view. Therein lies waiting a continuum of possibilities where autism is concerned. In a world besieged by hatred and intolerance for diversity—a world so leaden and slow to change—I finally understood. Completely.

PART I

Unlimited
Possibilities

one

The World Needs Autism

*"With one in 166 children being diagnosed
with autism, it can no longer be called rare.
We have an epidemic on our hands. Every 16
minutes, another child is diagnosed with
autism."*

—Julie Krasnow, *Indianapolis Star*

The world needs autism. Of this, I am convinced. The
world needs autism *now* more than ever. Don't believe
me? Look around...look closely and carefully. Contemplate a
global awareness. Consider the call to action we've received
in recent times by way of grand-scale, devastating natural disasters and international terrorist attacks, which drastically
spiked an online "rapture" index, a Christian speedometer
that measures how quickly the world is careening toward the
day of reckoning. Popular culture has relaxed ethical conduct
so much that films and television programming have desensi-
tized us to sex, violence, and abusive language to the point
where there is no more room to push the proverbial envelope.
Motion pictures such as *Saw* and its sequels, *Wolfcreek, The
Devil's Rejects, Turistas,* and *Hostel* have given rise to a pornographic
franchise: human beings mutilating other human beings with

~ 33

sadistic ardor in gratuitous, graphic depictions of torture. Witness, too, the celebrity behavior we have come to condone as acceptable due to "wardrobe malfunctions," racial rants, and sordid misconduct. Although this book was written during wartime, it is the irresponsible misbehavior of certain public figures that made top news. There is vague accountability and fewer repercussions in consequence for one's misdeeds, which may, in fact, be rewarded post "rehab." Further, the premise of most reality television is predicated upon lust, greed, manipulation, deceit, and the endeavor for physical beauty at all costs. Such cultural poison has anesthetized us to our own humanity.

Think people don't emulate what they see? A recent Associated Press article speculates there's an astounding drop in social etiquette—rudeness and amorality is on the rise. Corporate corruption has fostered employee disloyalty. E-mail has taken passive-aggressive interactions to new heights. The 2006 National Violent Crime Summit concluded that "crime is coming back" in a big way. *USA Today* recently cited an FBI estimate for a 94 percent increase in hate-crime attacks against persons with developmental disabilities. "Road rage" reports are a daily occurrence. "Happy slapping" has become the latest craze: someone physically accosts an unsuspecting victim while another perpetrator records the assault with a camera phone, and posts the attack online for all to see. Internet child sex predators are rampant, and child pornography has become more brutal, with the number of images depicting violent abuse rising fourfold since 2003. Americans are insulated with artificial complacency from heinous international human-rights violations perpetrated by megalomaniac dictators. Instead, self-absorbed and selfish behavior without consideration of others has become the norm, it would seem. A "messiah complex" has emerged; we have become a narcissistic society bent on gratifying our own needs because "it's all about me." Violators of this pursuit are perceived as rivals. *And it's autistics that, clinically, are defined, in part, as lacking empathy and social reciprocity!*

In early 2007, the Centers for Disease Control and Prevention revised its autism statistics from the previous tally of 1 in every 166 children (which excludes countless untabulated adults), now suggesting that the national figures are closer to 1 in every 150. But perhaps the reverse statistic signifies the greater epidemic: of every 150 individuals, 149 are "normal" or *neuro-typical!* We so dearly need people with autism and other differences—in their mild, unaffected manner—to lend balance to the world, and refocus us on what's truly important. Perhaps this principle resonates most with parents who have been obliged to undergo a personal transformation as a result of their child's diagnosis—parents who otherwise may have succumbed to the messiah complex. One mother confessed, "I think [autism] has humbled me. I think I'm a pretty good parent, and I can do that sort of stuff well; but with autism, that ego is taken down a few pegs. I think it has helped me be more accepting of people with disabilities. Not that I was a complete anti-handicapped person before, but now I think more in terms of what people can do."

Dwindling are the days of parental shame and self-deprecating guilt, as underscored by the mother who wrote, "Autism for me was a challenge not a defeat." A new evolution is compelling parents to reenvision their lives, to see clearly their own transcendence, and to hold greater hope for the future. This is supported by research such as the "Qualitative

Investigation of Changes in the Belief Systems of Families of Children with Autism or Down syndrome," a document that concludes, "Although parents may grapple with lost dreams, over time positive adaptations can occur in the form of changed world views concerning life and disability, and an appreciation of the positive contributions made by children to family members and society as a whole. Parents' experiences indicate the importance of hope and of seeing possibilities that lie ahead."

In conjunction with the shifts observed in the introduction, one parent rejoiced and opened her heart by telling her circle of parent-friends, "I was just thinking about all the reasons I am ticked that my child is autistic and then thought, you know, if autism had not happened to our family I would not have learned so many things! So many people I would have never known! I believe it has taught me courage beyond words. As much as I hate it, it has made me a better person and better parent to my child. Anyone here feel as though you were helped on some level by this diagnosis?" She received an avalanche of glowing responses, among them were the following:

> I find generally that I have a lot more patience, but what really is striking is that I am not intimidated by anything at work! People say, "Oh, this project is going to be hard" or, "This is difficult"—and inside I just laugh and think, hey, this is not difficult; everyone on this [message] board knows what difficult is. I find that I just don't fret about a lot of trivial things at work that I used to fret about.

Autism has made me a far less selfish, far braver person. Autism has taught me to value things that I ignored in the past. Autism has shown me the better side of human nature as I observe other parents moving Heaven and Earth for their children. Autism has, in some ways, brought my husband and me even closer together. Autism has made me see what's important in life, and it's not the pursuit of success and money. Autism has humbled me. And that's a good thing. Through autism, I've made some lifelong friendships. Autism has put my own character flaws in relief so that I can now address them. Autism has made me value my own health and what youth I have left, so I take much better care of myself. My son needs me to be healthy and energetic. Autism has made me into a far more organized person. Autism has forced me to become a better and more efficient housekeeper, so that at least some of life's chaos is under control. Autism made me finally grow up.

Autism made me understand that I'm not in control. Autism made me feel helpless, sad, and angry! It made me look to a Higher Power to find comfort, strength, order, and hope. And after finding these things, I can't say it was autism that made me a better person, but God—and finding Him—has been a tremendous positive! My marriage is better, I have my priorities straight, it has brought me closer to God, and I honestly think I am a much better person.

Life is what happens while you're making other plans—I forget who said it. I definitely had other plans. But my life is beautiful anyway. And God gives me little and huge blessings in each day to remind me of His love. Cardinals, flowers, [my son's] amazing sense of humor and intelligence, my daughter's sense of justice and hard work, our marriage, and friends. Somehow, I'm able to keep fighting my fears and keep going.

I know God has a purpose for all of us and I feel it would almost be—dare I say—a disgrace to not use *my* experience to be a *hope* and help to others. When I see my daughter's smile, especially on those "good days," I feel I can do anything, and what I want to do is to help others.

I am amazed at what God can do with a life. I have learned that nothing is impossible. No one could have told me a couple of years ago that we would be here. There are still issues to address, and educational needs to fight for, but God has given me the wisdom and strength at each and every step. I have learned that I don't have to follow anyone else's pattern or expectations.

Autism has made me more humble. It has made me put all my faith and trust in God and remember that this life leads to the next and that [my son] is my angel here on Earth. It has also helped me think "out of the box."

Autism has taught me the meaning of true love. I know you are supposed to use that phrase for a significant other in your life, but what I feel for my niece is the truest and purest love. Autism has taught me to be selfless, it has made me see the world in a different way, and it brings compassion and spirituality to my life. It makes me appreciate the small stuff, a beautiful smile from my niece when she sees me, the way she gets a kind of smirk when you tell her she has done a good job, or when she reaches up and puts her arms around me while we sit on the couch—there is nothing better than that in life. I would not be the same person that I am without autism in my world. All these children are angels; maybe their job is to make us all into better human beings.

———————

I feel privileged that God picked me and my husband— as he did all of you—to be parents to our kids. He knew that *we* would *love* them. The fact is that all of these children are *truly amazing.* They were born with some deficits, yes, but *look at all the gifts they have.* I look at nature and the beauty of it all because my son is obsessed with all things green and outdoors. I know that there truly is an "other side," because my son is attached to pictures of people he has never known (and will never know in this lifetime), but yet...he *knows* them. I stop and actually *see* where I'm going instead of just walking by.

———————

"Look at all the gifts they have." There are many autistics who are silently awaiting the opportunity to share their gifts with us. What kind of gifts? The same gifts and talents we all possess, but at higher degrees of vibration, particularly in relation to our senses. Isn't that one way to define us all uniquely—human beings functioning at different levels of vibration? It's the invisible equivalent of musical DNA. Consider that we may have not yet tapped unspoken wisdoms and truths unknown, not only from within ourselves, but from the inner sanctuary that dwells within the person with autism who lives in silence. And when you live in silence, you spend your time listening, processing, and very carefully observing—virtually a perpetual state of meditation. This is not so dissimilar from those of high-religious standing who intentionally undertake a vow of silence in order to attain a spiritual plane beyond what is typical. It is not unusual for people with autism to share their gifts in ways that some would define as spiritual and others would chalk up to mere coincidence. Well, coincidence may be so but, then, ultimately within the universal scheme, who do you think *invented* the very concept of coincidence? There is potential for us all to develop multisensory perceptive abilities in the way that a person who is blind has finely sharpened compensatory senses.

Deepak Chopra, internationally-renown spiritual practitioner, writes of a fascinating parallel that echoes the ethereal sensations of many on the autism spectrum who experience a disconnect from that which is physical:

> The five senses imprison us in ways that are unconscious and invisible. Years ago, I read accounts of congenitally blind

people who were given sight overnight thanks to inno-
vative surgery. On being exposed to light for the first
time, they were often completely disoriented. They wondered why people dragged black patches around with
them wherever they went (we call them shadows). If
asked how big a cow was standing a hundred yards away,
they'd guess 3 inches tall; stairs were frightening two-
dimensional ladders climbing straight up the wall. Sometimes these bizarre perceptions were so disturbing that
the newly sighted preferred to sit in the dark with their
eyes closed. Aren't we doing the same by clinging to the
world of the five senses?

I have yet to meet a person with autism who has not, in some
capacity, declared their desire to give back of themselves, to share
their gifts, and to teach others. In their gentle way—as befits
their nature—people with autism compel us to higher standards
of deference and respect for humanity. Being present with the
autistic individual requires us to be calm and refrain, to be *silent*
and truly listen. What do you suppose people with autism have
indicated they're here to teach? The most salient themes of the
human experience: tolerance, patience, sensitivity, compassion,
and, of course, unconditional love. These themes consistently
emerge in my work as a consultant no matter where I go.

We need people with autism in the numbers with which
they've increased, especially if we're to unite in a renaissance
for what is right and true and good and kind. It is coming. And
the next major human rights movement to shatter myths and
tear down walls of hate will be lead by those meek of voice,
but strong of will. The challenge is to counter the culture of
fear that persists.

Countering the Culture of Fear

Autism is an industry. As regrettable as that may sound, it is the truth. In addition to major charitable organizations, there are those who profit handsomely from scientific research-based methods, treatments, and programs that purport effectiveness as "clinically-proven" to remediate...recover...*cure* autism. To the parent hit like a ton of bricks by the diagnosis of autism, that's a powerful lure indeed. In chancing to grasp the brass ring of hope, some families have sacrificed everything—their homes, their jobs, their marriages—to financially provide their autistic child with what they are caused to believe is *the* answer. The "answer" usually comes in the form of an intensive, high-cost treatment program, one-on-one—adult specialist to child—for 25, 40, or more hours a week with the intent to suppress and extinguish autistic quirks, tics, and traits, while reinforcing new skills usually rewarded with an earned token, a favored activity, or piece of candy.

But compliance for the sake of compliance does not equal success; were this not true, we'd be deluged with the grown-up adulations of those autistics extolling the virtues of such uncompromising rituals from their childhood—and yet there are none. (To quote self-advocate Brian Henson, "Parents and professionals who constantly tell children how they ought to behave suffer from 'oughtism.'") If you are the autistic one engaged in a rigid regiment, your options are few. I can compel you to do what I want because I'm older than you are, I've asserted my control, and I've intimidated, coerced, or pressured you to comply. And the M&M, with its runny lacquer palmed in my unclean hand, is *not* an apt reward in exchange for your tolerance.

In our not-so-distant history of "managing" people's severe behaviors, there was a time when your risk for not complying wasn't the withholding of an M&M, but being physically restrained for indistinct periods, chemically restrained with sedating antipsychotic medication, being swatted over the head, having an ammonia capsule snapped open under your nostrils, being sprayed in the face with fox urine (yes, believe it), or punitively confined to seclusion. The manner in which "maladaptive behavior" was exorcised came with few limitations in an era when its victims were commonly called inmates and defectives.

Incredibly, the use of such aversives still occurs. Everytime I learn of a fresh incident of abuse, I think of the perpetrator: if only they knew the truth about autism, intellect, and spirituality. Instances of school children with autism being hit, kicked, pinched, locked in closets, strapped to chairs, and having their mouths taped shut occur with alarming frequency (see *www.neurodiversity.com/abuse.html* for details). And in May 2006, The Judge Rotenberg Center in Canton, Massachusetts, made news when it was reported that about half of its 250 students with developmental disabilities (including autism) were "fitted with electrodes on their arms and legs and specially wired backpacks that allow staff members to apply a 2-second [electric] jolt if they misbehave." Documented allegations filed by one attorney included the following atrocious indignities:

⊛   Shock was administered to the testicles of a
     young man named Jose causing the type of pain
     that no one should ever realize.

- A deaf child was regularly shocked for not listening to verbal instructions.

- One student was shocked a multiple amount of times, consecutively, for squinting.

- A student got out of her seat to go to the bathroom and was shocked; thereafter, a bowel movement was detected and the student was shocked again.

- A non-verbal, "severely retarded" student was consequated for moaning, which was her only means of communication.

- Students were tied down on boards and hours later were shocked repeatedly for behavior unrealized by the student.

- Indiscriminate, uncontrolled shock was administered mechanically to many students with no supervision at all.

- Students were burned in multiple areas of their bodies and the burns went unreported and sometimes untreated.

Such purported incidents are not relegated to the Rotenberg Center alone, and, according to news reports, "most families that send their children to the school support the limited use of shock therapy...." This is perhaps more shocking than the shocks themselves, which were compared to bee stings in one account, dispensed from a device formally called the Graduated Electronic Decelerator. The outrageous irony is that we would no sooner punish as contemptuous the involuntary tics, tremors, or spasms of those with Parkinson's, Cerebral Palsy, or Tourette's. Such permissiveness is not only symptomatic of our burgeoning cultural indifference, it is reflective of our historical absence of humane compassion for those deemed "different." Hence, there has been a total breakdown in communication between respectful best practice and compliance for the sake of obedience.

Don't most autistics thrive upon predictability, structure, and routine? Absolutely. But a strictly "outside-in" approach to managing and shaping someone into a model of conformity is not an equal partnership that begins with who they are, from where they stand. The automobile manufacturer creating a new mini-van targeting young families with small children wouldn't dare dream of going about their business without surveying a consumer focus group of the very persons for whom the new mini-van was being designed. In autism, the reverse approach is true—few glean information to develop best practices from the experts themselves, the very persons who experience the autism.

Further, many autistics can't transfer to real life that which they successfully reiterate back to a therapist, one-on-one in isolation—which has earned an M&M—because most autistics *don't think that way*; they retain information best by doing in the moment, and learning in real time, as perhaps you do, too. During drills, one young man was successfully taught to repeat back his house number in response to the question, "What's your address?" But when he eloped in to town, he could not answer the police officer who asked, "Where do you live?" because it wasn't the same thing.

I will better learn "apple" not from a flash card, but from *experiencing* "apple" with all my senses, assimilating its beingness in total form, at the orchard, grocery, or kitchen table. Remember this parable: I hear and I forget, I see and I know, I do and I understand. If this is a partnership—a pleasing collaboration—then I, as the autistic one, am likely to transcribe the apple event (embellished with glad tidings) in home-movie format for future replay in the film vault of my mind—without cause to upset the apple cart.

Develop a respectful relationship with me, the autistic individual—one that communicates reciprocal trust—*and* imbed elements of my most passionate special interest throughout learning opportunities (not abstain my passion as a reward *you* control), and *I will learn and grow*! Because I so love *The Wizard of Oz*, please don't disservice me by labeling it a compulsive obsession; *employ it* as a teaching tool to support my understanding of severe weather systems, farming and agriculture, hot air balloons, a certain breed of terrier, and counting configurations of yellow bricks—a continuum of possibilities await. It's *that* simple, and recent studies show such reciprocal relationship-based approaches are not only successful, but also cost-effective.

This is not rocket science, though there are those who would have you believe it is. Why? Because autism is an industry. A 2006 study authored by Michael Ganz, assistant professor of society, human development, and health at the Harvard School of Public Health, is the first to comprehensively survey and document the costs of supporting someone with autism in the United States. According to the study, it can cost about $3.2 million to take care of an autistic person throughout his or her lifetime; this translates into autism accruing costs of an estimated $35 billion per year to society. What Ganz defined as "direct costs" were broken down into medical costs (physician and outpatient services), prescription medication, and behavioral therapies (estimated to cost, on average, more than $29,000 per person per year). Direct non-medical costs factored in special education, camps, and child care, which Ganz estimates to cost more than $38,000 annually for those with "lower levels of disability," and exceed $43,000 for those with "higher levels."

Ganz's conclusions continue, "Indirect costs equal the value of lost productivity resulting from a person having autism, for example, the difference in potential income between someone with autism and someone without. It also captures the value of lost productivity for an autistic person's parents. Examples include loss of income due to reduced work hours or not working altogether." Annual indirect costs for persons with autism and their parents were ultimately estimated to range from more than $39,000 to nearly $130,000. (By comparison, the Rotenberg Center in Massachusetts is reported to receive $50 million annually to fund services for the 150 autistic and disabled students who attend from New York State.)

Transcendence Rising

Not only are these study results staggering, they're imposing—purposely so—intended to highlight disparity. And they assume that everyone requires "specialized," segregated, time-intensive, and costly services. This has raised the ire of parents led to believe that more is better. A November 2006 *Newsweek* article incited one father to bemoan a "'cure' mindset, which relies on pseudoscience and fear mongering.'

Perhaps *Newsweek* can follow up with an article about the real autism epidemic—the burgeoning quack cure industry, and the unethical providers who drain parents' resources with false promises."

"No one can tell me that the two hours of Applied Behavioral Analysis (ABA) is not helping Liam," conceded a mom who opts for a natural, flow-within-the-day approach. "I see it with my own two eyes. I follow through, and we live day-to-day life in a 'verbal ABA' style. I ask my therapist lots of questions. If she is working on a certain sign and limiting tantrums, I work on that as well all week. I believe my son is better off with two hours than none. It is so obvious for us. Yes, he would benefit with more hours, but I would never stop because it is not the recommended number of hours. Sorry, that is B.S...all of this stuff feeds on mommy-guilt and makes some of us feel as if our children are doomed if they don't get 25 hours of ABA." Still, the dangling carrot of recovery looms for many. In a May 23, 2006, open letter to the Schafer Autism Report, an Internet news service, Maureen Monihan adopted a realistic reflection based on experience:

> I do know two children who recovered through intensive ABA. But, I know far more parents who tried everything. Some of their children never made any progress. Many of these children are doing very well, but definitely still have autism. We are so far from "recovery" being reality for most children. There is so much more research that needs to be done, both in how to prevent autism and how to help the majority of people who will always have autism live better lives. Maybe parents of newly-diagnosed children need to believe in "recovery" in order

to find the energy to do all they can to help their child,
but even today, most parents will never return to that
before life. We have made progress in 10 years, but not
that much.

Terry Walker, an adult with Asperger's Syndrome, advocates the alternative. Instead of the movement for erasing all
traces of one's autism, Walker stresses a shift that implores
our culture to embrace diversity. "That's why I opt for chang-
ing the world around me," Walker says. "I think that does more
good long-term."

So why is hardly anyone listening? Why is no one adopting the mini-van approach that values persons with autism as
equal partners in planning? Surely this is the proper response
to supporting the autistic individual; there are two reasons
why this does not occur. First, few people want to hear from
autistic self-advocates. Tokenism exists. It is shown by who is
solicited to keynote a conference, or serve on an advisory
board; it's politically correct to ensure representation this way.
But when the rubber meets the road, persons with autism are
not self-determining the very systems that propose to serve
them. Why on earth not? Aren't they the keepers of untapped
insights that could prove beneficial in developing autism-
specific cultural competency? Of course, and if I am truly
professional and altruistic in my endeavors, I am compelled
to listen. But that also means I might not like what I hear.
And if enough self-advocates are united in saying the same
thing, I'm obliged to either refute or unveil my misgivings, conceiv-
ably to alter the way I do business—to some, that's a threat,
not to mention potential loss of revenue.

"We need acceptance about who we are and the way we are. That means you have to get out of the cure mindset," says Joe Mele, an autism self-advocate, quoted in the *New York Times* article, "How About Not 'Curing' Us, Some Autistics Are Pleading." Jim Sinclair, who composed the 1993 essay, "Don't Mourn for Us," agrees about those who would wish to eradicate autism entirely. "What they're saying is their goal is to create a world that has no people like us in it." And Johnny Seitz, who used his intuitive abilities to aid Dick Clark in regaining the use of his muscles post-stroke, decries, "I do not need to be cured, I'm fine! We need to be accepted, maybe understood a little better, but not cured. We are not broken, we are different!" In reaction to the tragic, stereotyped media spins on autism's afflicted "sufferers," high-schooler Justin Mulvaney bristles, "People don't suffer from Asperger's, they suffer because they're depressed from being left out and beat up all the time." Such harassment is what brought another teenager with autism to deduce, "Only God understands me."

As the events of spring 2006 continued to coincide, a triumvirate of shocking incidents rocked the autism community. Days apart, parents took the lives of their autistic children. Absent was an aura of acceptance, pathology vanquished; these sacrificial offerings were also borne of suffering, a hellish turmoil conceived of excruciating parental agony. In an unconditional utopia, the murders, attributed by one victim's grandmother to "end her pain and the pain of her daughter..." would've been avoidable, a non-issue. Instead, the murders were romanticized by one surviving relative as "an act of love" by a parent who had exhausted all means to "recover" her child into normalcy. It's not the first time it's happened;

unless we create a paradigm shift that assuages the unreasonable "recovery at any cost" myth—and absolves parental guilt ("If only I had done this, tried that...")—it surely won't be the last.

The second reason why self-advocates are not equal partners in the autism industry is that people are unpresuming of intellect. There is still a very prevalent stereotype that defines many people with autism as intellectually inferior, or mentally retarded, and incapable of contributing, seen as nothing more than "trainable," possibly "educable." The 2006 *Newsweek* story on transitioning to adulthood brought this retort from a 42-year-old man with autism: "What happens when autistics grow up? Why not ask an adult autistic? Nowhere does the article talk about autistics who are now adults. It seems that not only are we ignored by organizations which claim to advocate for us, but by the media as well. Perhaps the author believes we're all in institutions, or that we have nothing important to contribute, but the overall effect is that we're treated as though we don't exist."

Julia, a mom passionate to make the case for presumption of intellect, summed it up so beautifully after being inspired by my works:

> The point is to always presume intellect in your child. What this means is just because your child is non-verbal or severely autistic, don't *assume* that this means your child is not capable of *understanding, thinking,* and *feeling.* A lot of parents, and people in society, make the *huge mistake* of thinking that just because a child is autistic, and/or non-verbal, that they must be "ignorant," "stupid," or otherwise. They talk down to them and "over them."

Any child with a delay may have deficits in areas that we wish were not so, but this does not mean that the child is not smart or not able to comprehend. Think of a deaf person for example; do we consider them to be less intelligent because they are not able to hear? A person who has had a stroke may not be able to tell you what they want, but they sure can understand what you say. If your child is not mentally retarded (and many if not the majority of autistics are not), then you should always presume intelligence and treat them as such. The following is a checklist to help decipher what you should be doing:

- Talk to your child as if he *was* neuro-typical.

- Just because he may not act or speak the way you wish he would, it doesn't mean he doesn't understand what you say and how you say it.

- *All children* deserve to develop their own personality; sure, therapy can help with speech and behavioral issues, but autism is part of who your child is and that will never change. Accept it and accept them for *who they are, not who you want them to be.*

- Applaud what they can do. We hear so much of what our children can't and won't do; how about what they *can* do. My child may not pronounce words correctly, but he is very musically inclined and loves nature. He's a *great helper*—he helps water the "flawahs" and opens cupboard doors when I ask him to. He points to his shoes when he wants them off. He gives hugs, he laughs at

> funny stuff, he says "ouch" when he falls down.
> These are *great things*.
>
> So much time is spent on the deficits of this disorder
> that we, as parents, sometimes forget that our children
> are still human beings with thoughts, feelings, and emotions.
> They may not be able to express them to us in the way
> that we want, but they still need to be heard in their own
> voice. I'm not bashing anyone, I just think we *all* (me
> included) need to remember that.

Toni, a New York State mom, knows autism intimately and echoes Julia's vision. Mother to a son and stepson with autism, and wife to a man with Asperger's, Toni considers the dramatically unaccountable rise in autism with a prophecy for the future. "Twenty or 30 years from now there may be more autistic people than non-autistic people. The children who will become the leaders of tomorrow will more likely than not be autistic and will possess the traits of greatness...autism is evolution!"

Considering that males are four to five times more likely to be autistic, the implication suggests a softening of aggression in this gender, inaugurating a world at peace. Toni's foresight also evokes the Biblical Beatitude, "Blessed are the meek for they shall inherit the earth," further implying not evolution but *revolution*. And if studies conducted during a 20-year period by the German Psychological Association, that reflect an increasingly less-sensitive, more-dangerous culture with each succeeding generation, are valid, the autism revolution is transpiring not a moment too soon. We are in the midst of a spiritual renaissance, a time in which we all have the potential to learn and grow from one another. If you leaf through an old family photo album or view a childhood home movie, you'll see yourself as an infant, a toddler, a teen. Even though you have "morphed" physically in ways that are very different, you are still you—you've never *not* been you, even in the infant's body. We can collectively expand our thinking—our consciousness—in ways that are similar through opportunities to demonstrate a renewed respect and an enhanced courtesy, not only for persons with disabilities, but for each other.

A New Humanity

Carol attended one of my autism presentations during which I set the tone by espousing these principles. She understood implicitly the power of seeking forgiveness as a byproduct of presuming intellect by making atonement for her unbecoming past behavior. She graciously shares her glorious awakening for us all:

> My younger sister, Sally, was born in 1958. Up until age 2 1/2, Sally appeared to develop normally. She had acquired some speech and was interacting with everyone in the family. My parents first got concerned when Sally slowly lost her speech and began to exhibit some unusual mannerisms. The family physician referred them to a large hospital in New Jersey that had a special diagnostic program. Sally was diagnosed with severe mental retardation.
>
> Sally and I were very close throughout our childhood, even sharing a room together. Somehow, I always had the sense that there was "more" to her than she could

communicate. Sally was finally given the opportunity to go to school at age 9, when the right to education became a law, but her behaviors grew more and more challenging. At times she was quite aggressive. My parents struggled to do the best they could, but family life was challenging. Having friends over was difficult at best, and we were never able to go anywhere as a family because there was always concern that Sally would have a tantrum. Babysitters were out of the question.

When Sally was 16, things really got difficult. Although I had learned through the years how to soothe Sally, she was physically aggressive toward my mother. I broke up many physical altercations. After a particularly difficult period, my parents were so overwhelmed that they arranged placement for Sally at a state center for the mentally retarded.

For years, my parents visited Sally and had her home for weekends. But her behavior led to several psychiatric hospitalizations; the prescribed medications were not helpful. Sally was so upset when she needed to return to the state center after a visit, that she fought my parents all the way to the door. Although I tried to remain part of Sally's life during this time, the situation was heartbreaking. Eventually, my parents and I stopped seeing Sally. We simply couldn't handle it.

Throughout those 12 years of no contact, I felt terrible guilt, especially because I had made my career working with disabled people. Eventually in 2004, I decided that I wanted and needed to try to be part of Sally's life again. (I think that I had finally grown to a point where I thought I could deal with the emotion of the situation.) I made arrangements to visit Sally. Because I was very anxious about the visit, my husband (who had only met Sally a few times), agreed to accompany me.

During the visit, Sally did not acknowledge me. She did not look at me or give any response that would indicate that she was pleased to see me. On the way home, my husband shared that he did not think that Sally knew who I was. I was devastated, but somehow knew that this was not the case.

A month later, I visited Sally again and we went out for ice cream. She again did not respond to me and made no eye contact. I felt terrible. In despair, I found myself sharing my feelings with her. I told her that I was so very sorry for not being part of her life. I told her that I simply could not handle it at the time. I told her that I really hoped that we could again be close and that I could be part of her life. Honestly, I did not expect her to respond. But after sitting quietly for a minute or so, Sally raised her eyes to look at me. She looked deeply into my eyes for what seemed a long time (but was probably only 15 seconds). I told her that I would do my best not to let her down. I knew she understood. I reached for her hand and she responded.

As I spent time with my sister, it was again clear to me that there is much "more" to Sally than she can communicate. At the first annual Team Review Meeting I attended at the state center with my sister, a young psychologist was present. His report was brief—he had seen Sally, and reconfirmed her diagnosis of severe mental retardation. Later, we struck up a conversation and he told me that he didn't know whether his evaluation really reflected Sally's abilities. He shared that during the session with my sister, he remarked to someone else in the room that it was very warm, that he was very thirsty, and that he wondered if there was anywhere he could get a soda. Shortly after, Sally stood up and left the room despite his request that she stay. He assumed that she had just wandered off. A couple of minutes later, he was surprised when Sally returned carrying a can of soda, which she handed to him. I asked him if he thought this behavior was consistent with a diagnosis of severe mental retardation. He agreed that it was not and I told him that I had long questioned the mental retardation diagnosis. I told him that I suspected my sister was autistic. After some thought, he said that he was not too familiar with autism spectrum disorders, but that he would like to talk with another psychologist at the center to determine whether that person could evaluate Sally. The results of the new evaluation clearly indicate that Sally is on the autism spectrum and that the extent of mental retardation (if any) is unclear.

Sally and I now share time together and she has joined us on a family vacation to the shore and for holiday periods. Sally often makes eye contact and even shares occasional smiles or giggles. We are working to discover better ways to communicate. I am blessed to be close with my sister again, and I know that she has forgiven me.

Carol's story illustrates how inordinately forgiving and patient so many people with autism can be when true love is at work. As you can see, it's never too late to repair and restore damaged relationships that were a result of being unpresuming of intellect, and not interacting with a belief in one's competence. It is only the beginning, for this pathway leads to higher ground—the opportunity for spiritual bonding beyond what we might imagine. Deepak Chopra summarizes our human potential for that which is natural, not supernatural—abilities presently inherent, yet dormant and untapped, in the many autistics who await our enrollment as equal partners:

> As our favor for solid, concrete things fades away, certain fringe phenomena will become our everyday. Healing without touch will be legitimized, because altering the field can alter the human body. Telepathy and clairvoyance will seem ordinary, because time and distance are compressed to a single point in the field; intuition and epiphanies will be explained as subtle field interactions. The best outcome would be that wisdom will reemerge as a vital human capacity, for there is no doubt that our spiritual forebears were deeply in touch with the same invisible reality that still surrounds us. We have shut out that reality in our stubborn, rigid insistence on believing our senses, but seeing with the eyes of the soul is possible. In the end, a new humanity is also possible once we escape the prison to which we have sentenced ourselves for far too long. The so-called sixth sense isn't a separate sense at all, but a new opening for human evolution with unlimited possibilities.

In contrast with the autism spectrum, a school psychologist, responding to my research, wrote, "The word autism has been given power; too much power and in the wrong ways....Too often we create pathology by focusing on deficits rather than the abundant spiritual gifts. The universe of consciousness is large; we as humans take very small pieces of that largeness and define that as reality. We need to open to greater possibilities."

This concept brought to mind an experience I had in which I found myself interacting with a father who had been led to believe the "pathology of deficits."

A monthly meeting for a group of mostly non-verbal adults with autism had just concluded in the community center room in which we met. A birthday party was scheduled in the room immediately following us, and as we were wrapping up, a dad with three children entered the room early. One of the children was a small boy with Down syndrome. From across the room, this youngster made a bee-line directly for me, threw his arms about my waist, and embraced me with magnanimous exuberance. I knelt beside him as his dad followed up behind. I pulled out my paper keyboard and said to the boy, "Perhaps you recognize these letters from *Sesame Street*." Without hesitation, the father hastily interjected, "Oh no, he's *profoundly retarded*." My reply was just as emphatic, "Oh, I don't pay much attention to those kinds of labels." I continued, "Do you see the people in this room?" I asked as we surveyed the group of autistics, some of whom were twirling, rocking, and making errant vocalizations. "Many of them have presented at conferences or have even been published, and most of them carry the label of 'retarded.'" The man's mouth hung open and his eyes grew wide with surprise. I'd like to think it was a spiritual *a-ha!* moment for him about possibilities and potential for the son whose intellect had already been written off needlessly.

Readers often mistake my writings as focused on children only; it is not so. I'm exploring spiritual concepts as related to all persons on the autism spectrum, including adults. In fact, akin to myself, it would seem that there exists a predisposition for similarly-affected adults to have an interest in such topics. In an April-2006 online poll of persons with Asperger's Syndrome at *Wrongplanet.net*, 75 percent of those who responded indicated a long-standing intrigue with the unexplained. One individual put it into perspective by stating, "'Paranormal' and 'supernatural' are just words describing phenomena *not yet* considered normal or natural. Stuff that makes people go, 'Well, that's simply not possible.' Speech was once paranormal, but is today quite normal. So were flight, space travel, x-rays, binoculars, and photographic memory. As soon as a certain number of people start exercising a habit or technology, it ceases being supernatural."

The resistance of some to think beyond conventional boundaries may be attributed to an unease between matters of spirituality and traditional science, to which Jaime Licauco, president of the Inner Mind Development Institute, responds:

> I see no conflict nor incompatibility between religion and paranormal phenomena. As a matter of fact, all religions, whether Buddhism, Islam, Hinduism, or Christianity, started with a paranormal phenomenon, with a vision or contact with a supernatural or divine being.... I think the problem lies in the erroneous assumption, especially by Christian religious authorities, that everything that is paranormal or supernatural must come from a dark side.

This is not true at all. Even Jesus Christ performed so many paranormal wonders, such as when he predicted the future, read people's minds, healed the sick, walked on water, changed water into wine, and revived the dead. Calling them miracles does not change their paranormal nature.... So, consciousness, the spiritual, and the mystical are considered outside the scope of materialist science. But true science should encompass all of reality, should it not?

And it would seem that all of reality is oftentimes availed to those sensitively susceptible, as with certain persons with autism. Consider the stratospheric, vibrational intensity of one young acquaintance who produces "paranormal wonders"— as yet unrefined—related by his mother:

> We found out about three years ago at a course by the Institute for Achievement of Human Potential that they know about children who are able to hear sounds most people cannot hear. Out of curiosity, we asked Colin if he could hear things that we couldn't. He mentioned turned off appliances, the garage door opener, halogen lights, and police radio. We were surprised to hear the radio part, and asked him about it. He wrote on his Facilitated Communication (FC) card that it was indeed the cause for some of his emotional crying spells he had in those days—he hears the horrible messages ambulances, firefighters, or police send. Due to his strong empathy with human beings, he just would break out in tears at times. Here are two stories we could somewhat verify.
>
> One was a deadly car accident not too far from where we live. He suddenly started crying—moments later we

heard the sirens from the fire station. When asked what was wrong with him, he said that there was an accident on Route 100, and someone had been killed. He also described some of the details the officials were saying on the radio, like an almost decapitated victim. It took Colin a while to settle down. The second story was of a more harmless nature. We were driving in our car, and a police car raced passed us with sirens and flashlights. I said aloud to my husband that I wondered where he was going, but pretty much forgot about it afterward. When we got to our destination, I used the FC card with Colin for something and he wrote down, "Mom, what is a hit-and-run?" I asked him how he came up with this question, and he facilitated that the officers in the passing police car had talked about it. So that was proof enough for me.

Colin also used to be agitated close to hospitals, and he confirmed later that he would hear all the messages between ambulances and hospitals. Similar things happen in airports, but he kind of enjoys the pilots communicating with the tower.

Please know I do not profess to speak for—or about—*all* of those on the autistic spectrum; our life experiences are unique. Further, my intent is not to glorify autistics as "messengers of God." On the contrary, we *all* hold the capacity to employ our spiritual gifts in order to be of service to others through unlimited possibilities. But *how* we do it is what we may come to know from those who do it naturally. We have much to be learning from our autistic friends about Dr. Chopra's "new humanity." Let's begin.

two

The Dichotomy of Consciousness

*"No act of kindness, however small, is ever
wasted."*

—Aesop

Numerous individuals with autism report the sensation of being physically disconnected, and not fully integrated with their bodies. It may be difficult to understand the division in orientation that many autistics experience; that is, the compensation that exists when one's own body arbitrarily vetoes messages the brain sends it to act, to move, to speak. Under such conditions, coordination of the autistic one's limbs and muscles requires extreme, conscious, and willful effort that is erratic at best and, finally, exhausting in the end—one's physical shell begs for acute concentration to accomplish that which is facile and unconscious for those who are neuro-typical. (One autistic friend uses the analogy of feeling like "cement" when describing his body.) The fundamental tenet, "presume intellect," contends that, similar to the person with Cerebral Palsy, the individual with autism is possessed of a competence wholly intact. To outsiders, the one who is compromised appears severely impaired and may be mistakenly labeled with mental retardation, Tourette's syndrome, or even as uneducable.

Unless you live with a degenerative neuro-muscular condition—the palsy of unmitigated tics and tremors from Huntingdon's, Parkinson's, Multiple Sclerosis, or ALS, also known as Lou Gehrig's disease—you may be unable to relate. But you *have* endured a similar dysfunction in brain-body communication if you've ever awakened in the middle of the night to the unsettling realization that circulation to your arm has ceased, and your limb is now deadened or "asleep"; it is, for all intents and purposes, "cement:" And as much as your brain wills your recalcitrant member to *move*, it simply will not stir of its own accord. Now, imagine if you felt this same nighttime paralysis in more than one limb—or even your voice box—*and* someone was firmly imposing their expectation that you follow instructions and stay on task using the affected body parts. (Milder renditions occur when we block, stutter, or transpose spoken language unintentionally, or find ourselves unable to banish the song repetitively looping in our head.) I recall being berated by a high school gym teacher for my inability to execute a left-handed cartwheel. I could manage a barely passable right-handed version, but I could not enjoin my impervious limbs to transfer the same physical mechanics to the opposite side of my body.

To further illustrate, enact the following exercise during which you will experience an "autism," that is, a brain-body disconnect or misfire that precludes your body from achieving that which your brain is insisting it process. To begin, hold a paper tablet on top of your head with the tablet facing the ceiling, and in your dominant hand hold a writing implement. Next, have someone else read the following script at an uninterrupted, rapid pace without pausing. *You may not stop to look at what you're doing, and you must remain mute throughout.*

- ⊛ Start at the top of the paper and draw a small, round circle that will be the snowman's head.

- ⊛ Now, drop to the bottom of the paper and draw the large round base of the snowman's body.

- ⊛ Next go back up to the snowman's head and draw a black top hat on it.

- ⊛ In the void between the small and large circles, draw a medium-size circle that will be the snowman's torso.

- ⊛ Now go back up to the head, and on the right-hand side, draw a lump of coal for an eye.

- ⊛ On the left-hand side of the torso, draw a tree-branch arm that extends out into fingers holding a broomstick.

- ⊛ At the exact point at which the small and medium circles intersect, draw a scarf wrapped around the snowman's head with its tails flapping in the breeze to the right.

- ⊛ Draw another eye on the left-hand side of the head and exactly between the two eyes, draw a carrot nose.

- ❀ On the right-hand side of the torso, draw another tree-branch arm with a small bird—species of your choosing—perched precisely halfway up the arm.
- ❀ Draw a smiley-face mouth.
- ❀ Now draw a small fir tree on the ground to the left of the snowman.
- ❀ Stop what you are doing.
- ❀ You may now look upon your work of art.

After your mirth (or mortification) subsides—stemming from how *unlike* a snowman your depiction resembles—let's process what you were thinking and feeling during that exercise. Was your reaction frustration, petulance, and/or humiliation? Was it maddening to be unable to request directions to be repeated, or to ask your instructor to slow down? What about the utter confusion in receiving information in a sequence different from what would have been logical for you? If you gave up midway through, we'd label you "non-compliant" if you were someone developmentally disabled. What if the quality of your work was dependent upon a letter grade…or a paycheck? Even with out-of-sequence directions, your brain was still processing the information. Your extreme challenge was enforcing your body to operationalize, putting it on paper in a way that was unusual and uncomfortable—completely different from the way you are accustomed. This exercise was less about your thought process than it was about your physical failure to produce a simple line drawing.

Now, consider a reverse way of being that emphasizes *cerebral over physical* in the way that many autistics exist, unrestricted by the constraints of *ego*. Some of you may have attained this super-conscious state through prayer or meditation; others may have slipped into it while showering, gardening, enjoying a leisurely walk or jog, driving a familiar route, bedridden with malady, or just before drowsing—your mind is relaxed and on auto-pilot. You are no longer focused on the physical; that is, an awareness of one's body by accommodating or satiating its needs. Instead, you may be experiencing a stream of consciousness that requires no effort. You may receive infused, inspired thoughts and images, or you may have solved a problem through processing information in ways unique to this state of being. In fact, every day we abdicate great expanses of time for this purpose over which we have little control; it's called sleep, and the unexplainable need for sleep might be likened to a mandated meditation—dreams are not unlike spiritual visions. Our slumber compels us to an intrinsic silence akin to the monk, the guru, or the autistic one. It is a comparable echelon of cognizance that many believe survives the mortality of our physical body; an irrevocable shift in human dynamics attained through pure thought sans our shell.

Imagine if you habitually lived at this level of consciousness, largely detached from the physical, and in perpetual, dreamlike meditation, vibrating at a different frequency and interpreting your environment in kaleidoscopic shards. Now picture being on this plane, tapping an unending stream of consciousness that could be defined as spiritual, and having others constantly trying to wrench you back to Earth, back to reality, so that you will draw a snowman on top of your head to exacting perfection.

Please don't misquote me; I am not suggesting that we, as caregivers, permit the autistic one to drift aloft on this plane all day, every day; that's not real life for any one of us, and we all have obligations and responsibilities in order to be productive and contribute. But I am suggesting *compromise*. We should shepard our loved ones with autism to artfully tame and refine—not cure—their experience, where and when it is required, without forfeiting the emphasis on aesthetics and high thought because its been weaned out of them, extinguished in favor of "normalization." Should the latter be our endeavor, my fear is we will deaden the very sensitivities that cause our spiritual giftedness to thrive and flourish. *This* is to what Dr. Chopra is referring when he wrote, "We have shut out that reality in our stubborn, rigid insistence on believing our senses, but seeing with the eyes of the soul is possible."

States of Solitude

A Course in Miracles teaches a salient truth, "The memory of God comes to the quiet mind." In other words, connecting with God, or our spiritual selves, occurs in solitude sans attachment to the cluttered, incessant physical world. In his essay, "Solitude in the Faith Traditions," Reverend Clair McPherson defines solitude as "the deliberate and intentional practice of being alone." The word *autism* derives its root from the Greek term "autos," or "self." It implies a state of solitude in which one draws inward—similar to the concentric spiral of a snail shell or nautilus—becoming intrinsic, solitary in thought and deed. Curiously, the definition of the words *monastery* and *monk* stem from the same Greek word, meaning "alone" or "single." Earlier, I suggested that, where autism is concerned, an analogy may be drawn between autistics who live in silence and persons who take a vow of silence for spiritual communion and clarification. Reverend McPherson states that solitude is the *requirement* for such enlightenment. Indeed, the Native American Vision Quest is traditionally a singular venture, a rite of passage embarked upon for spiritual growth. Devoid of speech, a new lexicon emerges: one of thoughts and conjectures, images and icons. Such solitude would be idyllic if *everyone* endeavored to attain it—then we'd relate in an equable manner. But living in autistic silence is not a willful act, as "deliberate and intentional practice of being alone" suggests. For many muted with autism, a sense of authentic personhood seems unobtainable.

Barb Rentenbach, an author who has autism, has described her way of being as a desolate glacier where even autistics refuse to winter. Through discovering an alternative to speech, Barb found liberation—the compromise just inferred—from "a blisteringly painful and lengthy moratorium of hopelessness, prejudice, anger, uncontrollable behavior problems, fear, and profound loneliness." She concedes, "Words freed my purpose and tamed the torturous chaos. Yes, it is like living in chaos, I have termed it like a hell even." These two extremes set in motion a circular paradox that is difficult to fathom. On one hand, neuro-typical persons seeking fulfillment desire to enter into yogic solitude so as to reap its spiritual rewards, but in order to assimilate with the neuro-typical world, autistics must *emerge* from the very silence—what Barb Rentenbach calls "hell"—that enlightened neuro-typicals strive to attain! Is there neuro-typical compromise on this continuum, in the way we expect autistics to join with the "real" world (versus retreat within the concentric chambers of the nautilus)? Barb proposes resolve—a merging of human souls in truce—for anyone wishing to understand the existence of those who dwell in nomadic silence on the autistic glacier:

> We are not hiding. You search with limited senses and therefore our humanity is camouflaged to you. Be still. Be quiet. Be. We notice you on the glacier. We observe you completely. Language presentation is the barrier to our friendship—not sentience or intellect. We do not speak your language, but you can speak ours. Be still. Be quiet. Be. And now be with us. Our silent and invisible language is that easy to learn. Feel it? Welcome. Our friendship has begun.

A double-standard permeates how, where, and with whom we place spiritual value. We revere, admire, and are rendered awestruck by persons we have elevated to religious heights because of their convictions, which, by necessity, include absorbing periods of prayer, solitude, and contemplation (*kenosis*). Psychologist Ester Buchholz writes, "Contemplation is often described as the preferred mode for achieving spiritual peace, which is why journeys on the way to truth or salvation are undertaken alone." And Larry Dossey, MD conjures Barb Rentenbach's artic glacier when he maintains that "the classic parapsychology studies that mention prayer explicitly are but the tip of a gigantic iceberg, and the data supporting the role of prayer is vaster than we have imagined." Dr. Dossey continues:

> Many religious folk are exceedingly uncomfortable about "parapsychology," and they deplore the practice of parapsychologists of equating prayer with mental intentionality, focused attention, concentration, or even meditation. They often feel that parapsychologists dishonor prayer and are disrespectful of the spiritual traditions in which prayer is embedded. I sympathize with these reservations; but after exploring prayer and parapsychology for several years, I feel that a clean separation between these fields does not exist, and is impossible to achieve. In experiments in parapsychology in which individuals attempt to influence living things at a distance, they often actually pray or enter a sacred, reverential, prayer-like state of mind to accomplish their task. On the other hand, when people pray, they often have paranormal experiences such as telepathy, clairvoyance, precognition, and so on. Anyone doubting this would do well to read philosopher Donald Evans' scholarly work, *Spirituality and Human Nature*, or historian Brian Inglis' classic book *Natural and Supernatural: A History of the Paranormal*."

Because we so infrequently presume their intellect, we are not beholden to those autistics who share as similar an existence as monks, nuns, gurus, and yogis, and who surely bear comparable fruits resulting from their own form of solitude; we, instead, focus on eliminating their pathology. The spiritual giftedness experienced *naturally* by some with autism isn't even recognized as "gifted" by those very persons, because it is second nature. Similar to Barb Rentenbach, these same persons may endure spiritual warfare with their own flesh—their very way of being—without cognizance of the opulence they offer, though making peace is in the offing.

Recently, I made the acquaintance of Carl, a 17-year-old young man with autism. To anyone unfamiliar with the autistic tenet "presume intellect," Carl might strike the casual observer as significantly impaired, someone either severely autistic or with Tourette's: he is seldom still except for brief periods, he makes repetitive motions, and he involuntarily blurts out fragments of speech or vocalizations. And yet Carl is full of grace unrecognized even by himself. A portion of Carl's day is spent in a local public school setting; the remainder is in a small classroom for children with autism operating out of a well-equipped trailer.

His mother, Elyse, is also his teacher, augmented by several teacher's aides. Elyse worked intensively with Carl to awaken the neural pathways that would enable his brain and body to collaborate in unison wherever possible. After using Facilitated Communication (FC) to type his "true think," as some autistics call it, Carl eventually began typing independently, sometimes requiring only gentle words from a trusted ally, or a loving prompt on his shoulder, in order to fully access his self-confidence. In the beginning (similar to so many with autism eager to please) Carl initially typed not his own thoughts, but those of his communication partners. To their chagrin, he would tap their subconscious and give that information, sometimes highly personal, as his response. Elyse and the teacher's aides kept quiet about it until finally opening up to one another to confirm their disquieting experiences.

From then on, assurances and encouragement to Carl were given with the caveat that he must draw from his own knowledge and his personal thoughts, not those of others. As his confidence advanced, Carl shed the need to "crib" answers from his trusted allies. One of Carl's classmates, a young girl who does not speak, was exhibiting what others would clinically dismiss as "non-compliant aggressive behaviors." The girl's behaviors confused and exasperated Elyse and the others who, through trial and error, were unsuccessful in discerning the root of their source. Through employing his spiritual gift, Carl was able to silently intuit his classmate's angst *directly from her*, and convey it to his staff in a way they would best understand. Once this information was shared—which was diametrically *opposed* to what Elyse had assumed was wrong—and the situation amended, the girl's "behaviors" ceased.

The young girl dwelled in a state of perpetual solitude; through knowing the state in which she dwelled—having dwelled there himself—Carl reached out to her in silence, as befits the way of the very gentle. But upon my asking Carl to "tell me about God," his reaction was visceral. He immediately typed the word *anger*, then he suddenly rose up and stalked to the window, his chest heaving as though he would hyperventilate. Once he was coaxed back to his place, I asked him to elaborate. Carl typed, "God has done nothing…" and, again, he stood up and paced off. Gently, I wondered if it was intended that he held God harmless, or if God had disappointed him, fell short of his expectations, hadn't "rescued" him. Carl completed the sentence, "God has done nothing to help me." I was taken aback. While I could certainly appreciate Carl's resentment for feeling abandoned, he was unable to comprehend that his spiritual gift was compensation from God, unique only to the most sensitive of beings. His way of being was not without purpose, his state of solitude had function. But that day, he would hear none of it.

Processing this over supper with a colleague from the local university, my head was spinning with the notion of unlimited possibilities. If Carl could willfully (or was it by permission?) enter into the solitude of another rendered mute, to serve as the interpreter, then we need a "Carl" in every major medical center in the country to relay the thoughts, wants, and desires of those in comas, those who have had strokes, those who have Alzheimer's, or any other debilitating condition that affects speech! Perhaps a "Carl" could even discern the fetus compromised in utero. Researchers at Pine Street Foundation in Sal Anselmo, California, use dogs to rightly discriminate cancer on patients' breath, so why not similarly procure autistic sensitivities *and* remunerate those so employed on par with physicians' salaries?

If this seems beyond the realm of probability, consider the late 2007 Boston University experiment that proposed the thoughts of a conscious man—but paralyzed for eight years and unable to speak—could be translated into speech via strategically implanted electrodes in his brain. I was anxious to share my brainstorm about Carl with Mary Ann, a retired special education teacher from Wisconsin who had years of interactions, including those intuitive and unspoken, with kids on the autism spectrum. "How do you think I wrote IEPs?" was Mary Ann's pat response. She explained that when it came time to compose Individualized Education Plans for students without speech, she gained perspective into their needs by requesting other students to glean relevant information from those who were mute, acting as intermediaries. Mary Ann said it was highly successful. When I suggested to her that this giftedness could be well employed to render service to strangers in dire need, Mary Ann cautioned my exuberance; it was not likely to work as I had envisioned. Something fundamental was lacking: a personal connection borne of compassion for the persons requiring intuiting. To wit, and above all else, love must be present.

PART II

Lessons
of the
Heart

three

Harmonious Patterns

> *"A heart is not judged by how much you love,*
> *but by how much you are loved by others."*
>
> —*The Wizard of Oz*

When I reflected upon Mary Ann's sobering admonition, I understood that, of course, it made good sense. Few among us experience incentive inspired to aid a total stranger in need without the presence of some sort of compassionate human connection (it's how we disassociate upon learning about lives lost for those we don't know). But such measure of purpose is precisely what induced Arizona native Tom Boyle's fatherly instincts to kick in as he witnessed a teenage bicyclist collide with a Camaro and become ensnared, bike and all, beneath its carriage as it dragged him for almost 30 feet. Most remarkable of all is that once the vehicle halted, Boyle *barehandedly hoisted* the front-end of the car—the average weight of which is more than 3,000 pounds—enabling the pinned boy to safely escape. For Boyle, the connection was made personal by his emotions in the moment. "All I could think is, what if that was my son," he said. "I'd want someone to do the same for him, to take the time and rub his head and make him feel good until help arrived."

In fact, this very principle was among the myriad explanations for the resounding failure of a three-year, $2.4-million study—the most comprehensive and rigorous of its kind—that tested the power of prayer. In early April 2006, the results of the study, funded mostly by the John Templeton Foundation under the direction of Harvard Medical School cardiologist, Dr. Herbert Benson, showed that prayers offered by strangers to those undergoing coronary bypass surgery in six different hospitals had absolutely no effect. The persons sending prayers only received first names and a last-name initial of those for whom they were instructed to pray. Consequently, patients who were not prayed for were found to recover no better than those who were sent prayers; patients who *knowingly* received prayers actually developed greater post-surgery complications, such as abnormal heart rhythms, heart attack, or even stroke.

Michael Shermer, writing for *eSkeptic*, an Internet newsletter, summarized the theological implications of the research. "The ultimate fallacy of all such studies is theological. If God is omniscient and omnipotent, He should not need to be reminded or inveigled that someone needs healing. Scientific prayer makes God a celestial lab rat, leading to bad science and worse religion." Still, it was the study's absence of intimate association between pray-er and pray-ee that piqued my attention. Characterized as a "cookie-cutter approach," the *quality* of prayer in the study may have been affected by the nebulous anonymity between parties.

The type of prayer called for by the study is intercessory prayer. As defined by spiritual practitioner, Larry Dossey, MD, "intercessory" derives from the Latin words *inter,* meaning "between," and *cedere*, meaning "to go." Dr. Dossey further explains, "Intercessory prayer is, therefore, a go-between—an effort to mediate on behalf of, or plead the case of, someone else. Intercessory prayer is often called 'distant' prayer, because the individual being prayed for is often remote from the person who is praying." There is nothing to suggest, though, that intercessory prayer is to be enacted void of personal connection. On the contrary, its power lies, perhaps, in the human bonds established between those who know one another as lovers, compatriots, brothers, and relations. In consideration of the prior discussion on Terri Schiavo and the dichotomy of consciousness, Kathy Callahan's book, *Unseen Hands & Unknown Hearts*, documents her own daughter's emergence from a perilous coma, a recovery attributed to the power of unified prayer. To further illustrate, here's another example of such symbiosis from Karen of Corcoran, California:

> I was driving home from shopping in another town with 6-year-old non-verbal John in the back seat, when my cell phone rang. It was my mother. She asked if it was safe to tell me some really bad news while I drove. I said okay. My dad had just died suddenly and unexpectedly. I cried all the way home. No one was home when I got there. I gave John his favorite food and continued to cry "alone" for 12 minutes or so. I prayed that God would

> send someone to comfort me. My husband was unreach-
> able at work, and no one else was home. I was feeling like
> my heart had been ripped out. As I continued to pray, all
> of a sudden I felt two arms around me. John was giving
> me my first hug. He had never done it before, and has
> never done it since without hand-over-hand direction.
> He held on for as long as it took for me to calm down in
> amazement as my sorrow turned to wonder and thanks.

It all now crystallized with certain clarity. *This* is how my friend Mary Ann was able to craft IEPs in concert with spiritually gifted students acting as "go-betweens" for fellow classmates. When I thought about it, I had experienced something similar myself, circa 1991, when I was employed by a human services agency that supported adults with disabilities in the community. One middle-aged woman, Lydia, was unable to speak, save for a few verbalizations to indicate yes or no. Because of our close relationship, she quickly developed a propensity for typing on a paper keyboard, and was soon able to contribute to her lifestyle planning, respond to doctor's questions, and provide unique insight into her housemates' behavior.

Lydia's attendance at the local adult workshop facility could be quite challenging to motivate. There, she was expected to engage in "work preparedness," demonstrating her capacity for paid productivity by sorting, counting, and organizing metal screws, washers, or other small items. Lydia was expected to do this not just once, but repeatedly...all day, every day. As she wasn't meeting quota, once Lydia finished the process, an aide would undo what she had done, and ask that she begin again. Not unexpectedly under the circumstances, there were numerous occasions when Lydia would exercise her independence by choosing to drop to the ground at the mention of leaving for the workshop.

One day, I stopped in to visit Lydia at work at the same time an independent surveyor was also present. The surveyor's purpose was, in part, to ascertain the contentment of the individuals who participated in the workshop's programming. Upon approaching Lydia, I offered to be the intercessory—the go-between—by facilitating her typing. Never one to censor an individual's communication, I read aloud Lydia's reply to the surveyor's inquiry about the quality of programming. "Get me out of this hell hole" was Lydia's succinct, direct, and to-the-point sentiment, one that she obviously entrusted me to communicate on her behalf, unedited.

Controversy quickly ignited as the authenticity of the statement immediately came under fire—as if it were expected that Lydia be nothing but blissfully satisfied in her present situation. When she was privately interviewed by typing with a stranger—a representative from the workshop agency's home office—Lydia recanted, and confessed how pleased and contented she was, indeed (though her behavior continued to show otherwise). I wasn't surprised, and, in my heart, I knew her original statement to me, her confidant, was Lydia's "true think."

Another statement about communication partners, recorded in *Autism and the God Connection*, made utter sense. In reflecting upon the degree of physical support he requires, an autistic man named Izzy typed, "I am not sure of the exact technical details of how to explain this, but I pick up on their heartbeat—this can be done with some people, not with all people—and then I am able to type and communicate."

This concept corresponds to research in the burgeoning field of neurocardiology, the study of the "brain" of the heart, systematized by the Institute of HeartMath, Boulder Creek, California. In his book, *The Biology of Transcendence*, author Joseph Chilton Pearce explains that the same neurotransmitters (such as serotonin, dopamine, and norepinephrine) found in the brain, which influence our consciousness, were also discovered to exist in the ganglia of the heart, which, through intricate internal networks, affect the body's tissues, muscle structure, and organs. However, as Pearce observes, ganglia that typically "interrupt" or interpret communication between the heart and the just-referenced body parts are "unmediated" when interfacing between the heart's neural structures and the emotional-cognitive portion of the brain. In other words, HeartMath's neurocardiology contends an ongoing "dialogue" or fluent exchange between our heart and brain exists *uninterrupted* through these neural pathways.

Moreover, harmonious patterns, called "entrainment," have been recorded when heart and brain frequencies synchronize their respective wave forms, something like matching up EKG and EEG readings. These synchronized wave forms can be aligned from one person to another. It is in this way that mothers bond with infants when breastfeeding, and lovers are euphorically exalted to simultaneous climax through frictional contact. Fleeting everyday examples include thinking of a loved one only to have them phone or e-mail in that instant, or simultaneously saying the same thing or laughing spontaneously with a fine friend—something to which no one else would be privy in the moment. It is this concept that underlies Sweden's 2006 Uppsala University study that indicates "infants learn to predict the actions of others around the time they learn to perform those actions themselves."

Entrainment—synchronous rhythm between hearts and minds united—is precisely what Izzy described was possible with *some* people. Entrainment was certainly the key to the manner in which Carl intuited his classmate's needs, or Mary Ann developed her educational curriculum. On another level, entrainment—and lack thereof—most certainly contributed to studies that proved or disproved the validity of Facilitated Communication. Entrainment underscores relationship-based approaches to supporting individuals with differences, allieships that accept our autistic friends as intellectual peers originating in the presumption of intellect. (Entrainment is, therefore, extinct in behavior control and management environments.) Doc Lew Childre, coauthor of *Teaching Children to Love*, concurs, "Harmonizing heart and brain through love is what can establish a complete intelligence, a complete self, where a child can look at life and realize there are no dead ends, there are always possibilities...." Such a fusion has been echoed repeatedly in the countless declarations of *love* I've received in nearness of those with autism. And I'm reminded of Michael's words, whom I quoted in the introduction, when he's advised, "If you want to know the rightness of something, ask yourself how it feels emotionally, not physically...to feel emotion is eternally based. It is the energy of which we are made."

It is most peculiar that the alleged markers for inducing autism are as diverse as its own spectrum (vaccines, middle-aged fathers, and nasal spray among them), yet each indicator manifests in identical symptoms—what are the odds! In aggressively pursuing the autism "cure," have we been praying for the wrong miracle? Let us disallow a lowering of expectations in favor of altering and fine-tuning our *relationships*. Our focus then shifts from what causes autism to what autism *causes*. Instead of an "epidemic," perhaps autism is one remedy for what ails the world. Just think of what may come if we integrate instead of remediate: a congress of minds, societies of healers, intuits, and prophets—a veritable colony of *heart savants*! Where autism and spiritual giftedness are concerned, the power of entrainment—the loving bond between persons divinely conjoined—warrants further exploration.

All You Need Is Love

Earlier, when discussing my friend Carl, I suggested that his solitude—and that of others like him—was not without function. This form of introspective, perpetual contemplation is what spiritual philosopher, Dr. Wayne Dyer, dubs "in-Spirit." Is this what is meant by the concept that God created man in His image; not a *literal* interpretation (that is, arms, legs, two eyes, and so on) but, instead, a reference to the very composition of the *soul*, the essence of being in-Spirit? When we are in-Spirit with others, we are, as Dr. Dyer advises, "Living in the same vibrational energy as our Source and attracting that energy in each other." If love is the tie that binds, then the formula of the following equation holds true: being metaphysically attuned (*in-Spirit*) + physiologically entrained (*in-love*) = harmonious patterns (*in-spired*) = unlimited possibilities (*in-finite*).

Now, let's learn how beautifully the preceding equation consummated in a real-life scenario involving a mother and her autistic son. This comes from Theresa, a California mom who was once perplexed by her son Andrew's spiritual giftedness. As you'll read, through love, they discovered how to naturally merge and expand their relationship into unlimited possibilities. Theresa writes:

> This last year, I've come to accept my son's special abilities. Andrew is 10 years old. From very early on, my son would act out my—and others'—worst fears. I would be at someone's home and think in my mind, "I hope he doesn't pull down the drapes." No sooner could I finish my thought, and he would walk over to the drapes and begin to swing on them like Tarzan. I was infuriated because I knew he could somehow hear my fear. It wasn't until about a year ago I truly came to terms with his abilities of audio clairvoyance (his ability to hear others' internal dialogue).
>
> At times, Andrew would get excited and maybe tantrum. My husband would tell him to chill. Andrew took this phrase and changed it to "Kill! Kill!" It would scare me. This child had very limited abilities to speak, and for him to walk around chanting "Kill! Kill!" could not be good.

One day at camp, the young man shadowing Andrew had spoke of attention-getting behaviors. I had just always seen Andrew as reacting to his environment; I didn't see him as trying to get attention. So on the drive home, I began to review in my head about what that would look like—was he trying to get attention? I thought about how Andrew would say "Kill! Kill!"—was he trying to get attention this way? This conversation took place completely in my head. Andrew suddenly sat up in the back seat, laughed, and said the words, "Chill! Chill!" for the first time.

This was a pivotal moment for Andrew and me. Since then, our very intuitive homeopath has identified it as "audio clairvoyance." All of a sudden, it was much clearer for me. Now I understand him on a much deeper level. Most of my communication with him is intuitive. It's really quite handy, especially in public where, in the past, there have been some quite dramatic scenes. Everyday we both learn a little more about what this gift is, and how he can use it to find his way. Most of the time he seems to not know where these messages are coming from. We do lessons—not in math and reading—but in how to acknowledge and attend to the messages he is receiving. The information flows so easily for him in this mostly unknown (to the average person) dimension of communication. He gets extremely overwhelmed in a crowded room. I've communicated to him (intuitively) to imagine a bubble around himself. Reassuring him that what is outside the bubble is not his, and he does not need to attend to it. This creates an obvious calm over him.

Every day he learns a little better how to regulate the information he receives. Everyday he feels a little better in his own skin. His need for sameness and control slowly drops away. I see his abilities not as supernatural, but just natural. Andrew somehow has direct access to the flow of intuitive communication. He doesn't need to tap into it. It just flows for him naturally; so much so that it has been a constant distraction for him.

There are certain people who he is drawn to instantly, and they are always the gentlest and kindest of people. It has helped me know instantly if a person in our life is someone we really want to spend time with. His empathy is the purest I have ever experienced with any person. Not that he is always empathetic, but when he is, it is truly a beautiful thing. He has enriched our lives in so many ways. I have learned to overcome judgment, developed patience beyond what I ever thought was humanly possible, and everyday I learn to develop and trust my own intuition.

If you want to get *really* "way out there" in taking this further, consider the research of Robert G. Jahn, professor of aerospace science and the dean, emeritus, department of mechanical and aerospace engineering at Princeton University. Professor Jahn is also former director of the now-defunct Princeton Engineering Anomalies Research (PEAR)

Laboratory. He has conducted experiments to explore whether entrained compassion—love—emanating from test subjects can affect the functioning of electronic, "random event" generators and similar devices. In successfully exerting mental will upon such a device, one of Dr. Jahn's subjects explained, "I simply fell in love with the machine." Dr. Larry Dossey summarizes Jahn's seemingly improbable, illogical trials:

> Experiences such as these are extremely common in [parapsychology] subjects. In them, love seems to function as a form of intercession—literally, a go-between—that unites the subject and the object being influenced. If love is crucial to the success of [parapsychology] experiments, and if "God is love," then the Almighty appears to be less nervous than some of Her followers about entering the parapsychology lab.

Do you think this falls into the realm of science fiction? Consider that in July 2006, 25-year-old Matthew Nagle, from Massachusetts, made news with the headline, "The Man Who Can Open His E-mails by Power of Thought." Matthew's spinal cord was severed in a vicious knifing, paralyzing him from the neck down. Dr. John Donoghue, of Brown University in Rhode Island, and Cyberkinetics Neurotechnology Systems, implanted Matthew with a 4-millimeter-square chip that "reads" impulses in the primary motor cortex of his brain— the brain region that would control movement if Matthew still had use of his limbs. The implant chip is fitted with 100 sensors that measure Matthew's brainwaves, record the activity, and transmit these signals to a computer that controls various devices. While the technology is cutting-edge, *it is obsolete without Matthew's mental commands acting in concert with his implant*. Just three months later, in what was described as "a symphony of expertise," a 14-year-old boy with epilepsy, in alliance with neurologists at Washington University in St. Louis, became the first teenager outfitted with a brain-machine data device (a variation on the EEG technique) that allowed him to play *Space Invaders*, a video game, using only his thoughts. The implication for the technology's future employ in persons compromised with communication deficits, such as autism, is imminent.

Compassionate Alignment

Even if Dr. Jahn's people-and-machine experiments strain credibility for some, there's no denying capacity for the synchronous alignment human beings convey to one another; however, this compassionate attribute may be indigenous to persons with developmental disabilities, as evidenced by this telling anecdote from Jennifer in Albuquerque, New Mexico. Jennifer works with a young autistic student named Danielle:

> I take Danielle out on outings. She had asked me to buy her the *Lion King* CD two years ago. Every time we are together and she plays this CD, there is one song that she loves to skip to. It says something similar to "…he lives in you and in me, and he watches over all we see." It never fails—during this song she looks at me, and holds up her index finger, and says "We are one."

As the aunt to a beloved nephew with autism, Nicki Fischer knows the autism spectrum intimately. Her nephew, Danny, has lead Nicki in many endeavors to reach out to the autism community. But it was a personal hardship which Nicki endured—and from which she successfully emerged—that may shed light upon human connections most autistics cannot articulate, when revisiting the dichotomy of consciousness:

> Many traditions have embraced the idea of using the mind to calm the body; I use the body to calm the mind. Between June 2000 and April 2003, I underwent two neck surgeries and one shoulder surgery, and was just about to have a fourth neck surgery in a three-year time span. I had to do something to try and help myself get rid of every toxic dysfunction and malfunctioning cellular memory.

> I created a process for helping the body achieve and maintain its natural state of balance. I had to learn to breathe in each area of my body that was stuck and holding on to negativity. I had to learn to feel the painful memories that were trapped in the cellular memory and let it go. This process took approximately two-and-a-half years to complete. Through Vibration Regulation Training (VRT), my vibrations are kept balanced, at homeostasis. My energy is balanced, and balance is preferred over imbalance. When your body stores dysfunctional cellular memories or malfunctioning behavior, then your body runs your mind, and the mind follows the body's directions. Your brain is very diligent and does what it is told.

The brain is a very effective and efficient organ; it not only follows your orders, it learns shortcuts to get you there even faster the next time. The mind is a thinking brain that is trying to negotiate with a non-thinking body. Body memory is automatic and does not require a thought, just a feeling. The negative body memory must be eliminated so that the body is at peace. Once the body is at peace and the mind is free to think—without the automatic body response trigger—the mind can then, and only then, fully control the body response to stress and pressure. Until the body is free of blockages and toxic memories, the mind is unable to control the automatic triggered behavior of what the sensitive body is feeling and interpreting, and ultimately protecting.

I do not have any blockages or negativity stored in my body and it allows me to stay at a very high frequency at all times. I stand with someone and my body is open to everything that the other person is feeling in their body, both negative and positive. Their negative cellular structure is pulled into my body very quickly. I've trained myself through VRT to remove the negativity immediately and send back clean, peaceful energy to replace the negativity. The reset process is very quick, and can sometimes be instantaneous depending on the level of sensitivity of the other person. With VRT, I regulate and reset body energy and vibrations back to homeostasis via entrainment.

Borne of necessity to alleviate piercing pain, Nicki's technique is now driven by compassion to serve others as an intercessory via accelerated vibrational alignment (in-Spirit); but hers was a conscious effort. Where some individuals with autism are concerned, similar high-vibration healing interactions may come intuitively, as explored in *Autism and the God Connection*, or may be cultivated as with Theresa and Andrew. And if autism naturally predisposes some autistics to exude love, and to function with spirituality atypical in *human* interaction, what about entrainment with other living things, such as the plant and animal kingdoms?

Julia, mom to son Adam, tells of her son's natural capacity for appealing to God's green Earth with a language unique to those harmoniously attuned. Julia reports that Adam's mysterious "chatter" fills him with elation, and appears to be a two-way interaction during which he practically embraces flowers and shrubs. Julia writes from their Virginia home:

> My son Adam, who is now 3 years old, was officially diagnosed with PDD (Pervasive Developmental Disorder) at the age of 2 1/2. Even though Adam is considered non-verbal, he does have receptive speech; he understands what you say to him. In addition to having an autism spectrum disorder, my son also has some pretty amazing gifts. Not only does Adam understand what people say, he also has the ability to project his thoughts into others. He is essentially non-verbal, but "talks" nonstop in his own little language with bits and pieces of English thrown in here and there.

He loves nature and everything outdoors; plants and bugs are his favorites. My son will look at a plant book (one for adults, mind you) and actually seem as though he's reading it. One favorite thing he likes is to plop down in front of plants, trees, bushes, and chatter. Normally this is not something I would pay much attention to, but I had ordered some begonia bulbs from his school's fundraiser. After planting them and watering them, a month went by and nothing. I dug them up, replanted them, and moved them around to various spots in the yard (they are in pots). Then I noticed my little one took a great interest in them after I moved them to the backyard. He's always helping me water plants, although he enjoys watering himself as well! Every day when we would go outside, he would sit in between these two pots and chatter, sometimes very loudly and very animatedly. Imagine my surprise when, not too long after this, my plants started sprouting and taking off. It seems that whenever Adam takes an interest in any plant or tree or bush—even the ones we've sprayed with weed killer to get rid of—they will flourish. Now my husband and I only let him "talk" to the plants that we want to keep.

It would seem as though Adam communicates adoration to his plants in a divine manner, and they respond to his secret summons—but *how* does it work? To understand, we might look to a more common area of autistic giftedness. In *Autism and the God Connection*, the concept of autistic "picture exchange"—swapping mental imagery—with horses, dogs, cats, and other creatures, is revealed and illustrated with compelling examples. I've gathered anecdotes of domesticated and feral animals inexplicably drawn to autistics for purposes unknown. It's lovely that these kinds of exchanges occur, and I continue to receive such stunning stories; but my curiosity alone refused to be placated with the knowledge that autistic-animal communication randomly transpires. I wouldn't be satisfied until I knew *what* the animals were saying—and the relevance, if any, it has for the rest of us.

four

Animal Axioms

"I wanted to talk to the animals like Dr. Doolittle."

—Jane Goodall, chimpanzee researcher

The story Hazel shared from her Dallas, Texas, home is very similar to those I receive from parents all over the country; in this instance, Hazel shared a photograph to substantiate her claim. It is a powerful image of a massive, hulking gorilla pressed against the window of its habitat as Andrew, Hazel's golden-haired, 2 1/2-year-old son—who is on the autism spectrum—looks on, unphased and undaunted, dwarfed by the gorilla's substantial presence; they are separated only by a plate of glass, upon which Andrew has the open palms of both hands firmly planted, as he looks on in wonderment. But in the picture, the intimidating simian appears calm, complacent—harmoniously entrained—in a pensive gaze exchanged with Andrew. Hazel explains:

> I took this picture at the Dallas Zoo. I have never seen anything like this before. The "connection" with Andrew

and the gorilla lasted for several minutes. Whenever anyone else would come up to see the ape, it would pound the glass and run off. When Andrew came up, he or she calmed down and approached. Andrew put his hand on the glass and so did the gorilla. They each gave eye contact for some time. *I* don't even get eye contact from Andrew. There were several people around and they couldn't believe it either!

Andrew has had similar experiences with other animals, namely our dog Beulah. Andrew practically lives outside. He spends most of his time with Beulah. One day I couldn't find him. I began to search, and panic set in. I looked in the backyard only to find them asleep together in the doghouse. Andrew is a bit of a late communicator, but he has always gotten Beulah to do whatever he wants.

Wherever we go, if there is an animal it finds him. About a year ago we had new neighbors move in across the street. Any time he would cry (sometimes that was often), their dog would escape from the backyard and come to him. They finally gave their dog away because they couldn't keep her in the yard.

Andrew doesn't yet have the language skills to tell of any impressions he may have exchanged with the gorilla, but others *are* able to illuminate upon this kind of unspoken reciprocation with creatures great and small. *Animals in Translation* author, Temple Grandin, herself a high-functioning autistic, believes "some autistic kids can understand what animals are thinking and feeling because, like animals, they can't rely on language to communicate. Their world is based on pictures and sounds, smells, tastes, and touch." What Grandin doesn't explore is *how* these interactions transpire; what would draw Andrew's ape to him and him alone?

Cindy Wenger isn't autistic, but she does know animals on a highly-intuitive level. Working as an internationally-renown animal communicator, Cindy explains the interactive process accessible to us all:

> I have been "communicating" with animals all my life, professionally for a decade. As I child, "knowing" what animals were trying to convey came so naturally that I did not think it unusual. It was only later in life, after being socialized out of that ability, that I rediscovered that all beings can, and do, communicate with one another.
>
> Animal Communication is the process by which impressions, thoughts, images, and feelings can be transmitted and received between beings of different species. Some call this a form of telepathy or two-way thought transference. In any case, it is truly a universal language. This form of communication is like carrying on a conversation about the past, present, or future.
>
> I have communicated with hundreds of animals (and their human companions) during the last 10 years. It is always informative, exciting, and very humbling. I always marvel at how animals exhibit those characteristics that are solely attributed to humans; courage, dignity, nobleness, and valor can be found in all of God's creatures.

For example, I received a phone call in March 2003 from a gentleman named Sheldon about his 8-year-old female English springer spaniel, Star. He was at his wit's end and I was basically his last resort: Star, was not eating, losing weight, despondent, and not responding to treatment that consisted of x-rays, ultrasounds, and sporadic antibiotic treatments. The vets were stumped with what was wrong with her. The stress was mounting for everyone concerned.

When I gently connected to Star, she was down-right miserable, and not real talkative. I relayed to her that her humans were very worried and feeling helpless. Once I connected with her physically, I immediately felt nausea, cramps, bloating, and inflammation in my lower intestine area resulting in chronic diarrhea. I am not a vet and do not diagnose or prescribe, however I was immediately empathetic to what she was feeling. Her personality had even changed because of what she was experiencing physically.

I relayed to Sheldon what I was getting from Star; he confirmed how she had changed. I also asked if he would consider one more test for her; that he should take her back to his vet and ask for him to check her intestinal tract to rule out IBD (Inflammatory Bowel Disease). Because I related so strongly to what Star was feeling, I felt very confident in suggesting that Sheldon do this for her. (I suffer from the same disease.)

Ironically I had recently received a copy of a newsletter I subscribe to, *Your Dog,* and they had an article on

IBD in dogs. I faxed Sheldon the information so he could read up on the disease, and also what was being prescribed for treatment. A week later I received a grateful letter from Sheldon: Star had *finally* been properly diagnosed...with IBD!

When I thought about Cindy's occupation, I recalled an unusual experience of my own with a displaced praying mantis. One autumn afternoon, I noticed the mantis trying in vain to climb up the vinyl-siding portion of my back-porch roof. The vinyl was too slick a surface for its struggling feelers and, desiring to be of assistance, I spied a nearby twig, which I extended to the mantis. To my delight, it readily accepted the twig as an alternative surface, and I hastily transported it to the overgrown hillside beyond my backyard. As I gently set the twig down, the stately mantis disembarked as if it had expected such an airflight would conclude just so. As I gazed on in admiration, I suddenly heard a crackling, crunching noise; the mantis had immediately seized hold of a passing beetle, and was steadily devouring the luckless insect alive! In my mind, I felt a measure of revulsion as the shell of its prey split apart. Its famished consumption complete, the mantis turned to stare at me, and I was impressed with the thought, "Would you have me eat something already dead?" It was a fluent and natural response to my mental query; while I don't know for certain that it originated from the mantis, when I reflected upon it, it did make sense knowing that so few creatures are scavengers of carrion.

The most celebrated animal communicator of all-time, and the greatest saint in world history by some, was the 13th-century friar, Francis of Assisi. St. Francis had an innate aptitude for solidarity with nature and the creatures that inhabit it, counseling animals—birds, fish, mammals—in the ways of the divine akin to the reverence held by Native Americans. Similar to St. Francis, are some autistics also capable of registering animals' feelings and emotions that translate into an alternative language? A clue may be found in a summation of St. Francis' giftedness, transcribed by Brother Wayne Teasdale in *The Mystic Heart*, "All creatures were instantly attracted to him because his ego never obstructed the flow of relating.... [This was] based on his relationship with God, his immense joy, and his deep perception of the unity and interconnection of all living beings, including flowers, trees, mountains, winds, water, air, and sun." Similarities may be discerned in the following two narratives exemplary of those I have gathered about autistic-animal relationships.

Paula from Peoria, Illinois, is mom to 10-year-old Sean. For years, she has noticed a certain magnetism that attracts animals to him, and she contributed an anecdote to *Autism and the God Connection* about the wild fawn she witnessed emerge from a wooded glade, trotting directly toward her son. At my request, she attempted to track him down to retrieve some specifics, particularly with regard to any creature-communication he receives. Sean's responses astonished Paula during her interview with him about the animals:

> To my surprise he says they do talk to him. I pressed him pretty hard on this to make sure he was not just talking about pretend. I told him he would not get in

trouble if he was just reporting pretend thoughts, and he said, "Will I be in trouble if they really do?" I said, "They really have communicated with you?" He claims yes. He says he does not remember everything from the past, but he said the deer in your book was scared and wanted to come closer to him for comfort and a kiss. He claims the ducks he fed one day wanted to play with him, and that another time a deer came close because she was in danger and wanted to feel safe. I also must tell you that last night we went over to my sister's house because she has a new puppy. The puppy wanted nothing to do with anyone else but Sean. She crawled into his lap, and, when she wasn't lying on him, she was jumping, licking, and biting at him to play.

Traci, of Opelousas, Louisiana, tells of her daughter Ashtyn's actual "conversations" with animals; the responses she receives from her beloved creatures gain for us additional detail and perspective about what animals may think and know:

Ashtyn is a 5-year-old with autism spectrum disorder, believed to be the Asperger's type. Ashtyn seems to believe she is an animal; when nervous, she becomes a horse. The horse seems to be her animal of choice, or her fascination. She started loving and imitating horses at age 2. She seems to be able to relate the most with this animal. She is very annoyed by the saddle on a horse and tells me often, "It is not necessary" or, "they do not need it."

We have become the owner of many animals since we noticed Ashtyn's love and respect for animals. I remember when Ashtyn was about 2 years old, I walked outside to find her curled up in the fetal position with our family dog, Wilson. He was curled up around her like she was his pup! She seemed unbothered by the dirt on the ground, and was content being with the dog.

We also had several instances when we have found her up close with wild animals. My husband, a hunter, remarked how he could not believe how close squirrels and wild birds will come to her. He takes her often on his hunting scout trips! She seems to understand that animals live and die, and never seems bothered by the dying part. She accepts death as, "part of the circle of life."

I first noticed that she seems to hear what the animals think and feel one afternoon when returning from the store. As our car pulled into the driveway, she saw our two pet dogs in the driveway coming to greet us. She remarked, "Mom, they want to know where we went today." I chuckled and told her to tell them we went to Wal-Mart! She stayed outdoors and explained the whole trip to Wal-Mart that day. Many times she will remark that her pet rabbits are cold and need a blanket. She also tells us that our new puppy misses his mother and wants to know where his mother is. She has great insight on how they feel, either happy or sad. For the most part, she will tell me that animals are happy, but need more attention. The only animal that is sad is our pet dog, Dakota, who is very old. We just cannot make him happy! She knows he will die soon, and is eager for that to happen almost as though he is suffering a lot. (Well, the dog has arthritis, so she is right.)

Much of the time she is talking to the animals in a soft voice, and when I ask what she is saying, she says, "I am speaking to the dog." It is almost like she is sharing a secret, and the animal shares with her too. I have never met an animal that did not like her. I do think that she feels as though what she knows is sacred. It almost seems as though she is thinking deeply about what she knows.

She told me that when we went to the zoo last time, she heard monkeys speak to her through the cage. This would explain her wanting to go back to them over and over that day. She told me that they were not making much sense to her, and were speaking about things hard to understand. She did a little imitation for me that seemed to look much like a person that has lost their mind, needing to be in a mental hospital. She seemed to insist that the monkeys were sick, and that is why they talked this way! I thought maybe that since they were caged, she was trying to tell me that they were losing their minds somehow.

Last night we were at our relatives' house. Ashtyn wandered toward the fence, which keeps cattle in one certain area. She stood there staring at them as she always does. Many will walk right up to her and stare back. I asked her, "What do you think the cattle want to tell us today?" She never took her eyes off of them, but said, "Good-bye, they are saying good-bye!" She told me that as if she was stating something I should have known! Then she was done; I could not get her to say anymore. [Traci found out days later that these cattle were all scheduled to be slaughtered!]

Ashtyn was up early this morning making squeaking (high-pitched) sounds while laughing and playing with her new puppy. She started talking, and I listened, and this is what I found out. She says that not all animals speak. Only some of them do. Her new puppy speaks because he told her that he loves her this morning. She even imitated the tone of her puppy's voice for me, which sounds similar to an average 3-year-old. Ashtyn has always made the squeaking noises when playing with animals. She cannot whistle, and I guess this is how she makes up for that. It sounds akin to the sounds that dolphins make.

She continued to say that all of her pets talk to her, and this is because they are happy. Most animals that do not speak are sad, or they are hurting and have broken bones. She also said that other creatures speak as well. I asked her which creatures. Her response was, "Duh, Mom, butterflies of course!" She even imitated one for me with her voice. She said it was one that spoke to her. It was a very cheerful tone of voice. She said that it only told her "Hello!" She said that for the animals that do not speak, the way they communicate is through what she called "howling," which sounds like an animal in pain. She talked much about this, and then quickly changed the subject and said, "Let me get the coffee made now!"

She also told me that her puppy gets excited because he wants to know that we love him too, and he will know if I pick him up and hold him once in a while! Ashtyn's eyes were barely open this morning, and she was getting out of the bed to check on her puppy to see why he was crying. She then told me without being able to see his dog bowl, "He needs food in his bowl." I was shocked to find the bowl empty. There is no way she could see that from where she was standing—it was nearly in the other room! I was shocked!

I believe many of our own pets instinctively practice entrainment (remember, they, too, exist in a state of solitude). It is in this way that they seem to just *know* how to comfort and soothe us, and provide us with unconditional affection when we are ill, depressed, or distressed. When we have to be cautious about saying—or even *spelling*—certain words because of the reaction they'll incite, is it because our pets possess word recognition, or because, similar to Ashtyn, they are in a harmonious pattern so completely aligned with us? Is there, as Cindy Wenger contends, a universal "animalspeak"?

Genene, a friend familiar with my work, told me, "I recently spoke with a family friend whose son, Trey, is autistic. I mentioned some things from your book. Trey's mom then opened up to share what happens when Trey visits the dolphin exhibit at Chicago's Brookfield Zoo. The dolphins always approach Trey when he peers through the glass aquarium. The dolphins linger and nod and chat with him." I wondered about this as I contemplated Traci's description of Ashtyn's clandestine language: "It sounds much like the sounds that dolphins make." To understand further, I began my research by pursuing the one mammal on the cetacean order best known for its healing interactions with human beings and, especially, autistics: the *delphinidae*. And, as I discovered, if ever human beings had an aquatic mirror image, it would be reflected in this highly-intelligent creature. Not surprisingly, the word *entrainment* surfaced in my review of the literature.

The Voice of the Dolphin

To begin, I ordered Patricia St. John's 1991 book *The Secret Language of Dolphins* through inter-library loan. The narrative documents St. John's passion to assimilate unspoken knowledge and cues from the dolphins with whom she developed respectful, intuitive relationships; in time, she successfully applied this technique to her work with autistic children—respectful interactions without using spoken words, and in some cases, she contends, telepathy.

Similar to Nicki Fischer's experience of regulating her mind using her body, Patricia St. John attributes her spiritual growth to mastering control of her body using her *mind*—not unlike the dichotomy of consciousness of which I spoke earlier. In St. John's instance, she was able to willfully regulate her senses because her vision was deprived in childhood due to an ocular anomaly. She developed "extended sensory perception"—a phrase she prefers instead of ESP—or Heightened Perceptual Awareness (HPA), what St. John defines as "perceptions, or senses, that were strengthened to meet the demand for survival." Not only did St. John always have a fascination with the unexplained, her newfound ability to perceive with her senses beyond the average person is not unlike those with autism, a parallel she, herself, concludes. In fact, St. John also compares the supreme, non-verbal communication of dolphins with that of autistics when she writes:

> In years to come, the one comment I would hear most often about autistic children was that they try to block out the world around them and they don't, or won't, communicate...I found this statement to be totally, absolutely incorrect. Instead, I saw that autistics, like dolphins, were constantly bombarded with sensory input, constantly attempting to communicate with others, and more attuned to their environment and the people in it, than most other humans. Their approach to living, again like the dolphins, was more basic, more survival-oriented. The information they were constantly receiving was telling them how to act or react in situations, without any social restrictions accepted by them at the same time.

Patricia St. John addresses the aspect of spiritual giftedness in her work, noting the deep, penetrating stare from her dolphin comrades that look through and into her, not unlike the manner in which some autistic individuals discern allies versus adversaries. St. John also writes of the presumption of intellect in both the dolphins and the two autistic children she befriends; the former enact her verbal instructions upon her peer-to-peer requests, and the latter revealed when one mute young girl, Beth, begins to self-advocate in penciled long-hand, "Some people don't deduct I can read and I despise their doubting me." St. John goes on to make further comparisons between the clicking sounds and repetitive weaving and circling of the dolphins with autistic perseverations—which she rightfully advises is the result of an intelligence unchallenged, "What if progress, not repetition, was one of the answers of the problem of the lack of a lengthy attention span?...We communicated too slowly for [autistics]."

Indeed, similar to the competence concealed within many autistics, we may be unknowing of just *how* intelligent dolphins truly are. The late researcher, John C. Lilly, MD (whose work inspired the films *Day of the Dolphin* and *Altered States*), was enthralled with studying human consciousness and dolphin consciousness as evidenced in his books *Man and Dolphin* and *Lilly on Dolphins: Humans of the Sea*. In light of the intellectual capacity of dolphins and other cetaceans, Lilly noted, "They [cetaceans] have been on the planet now with brains our size or larger for 25 million years. We've only been here with our present brain size about two-tenths of a million years. So they've been here something on the order of 25 to 50 to 100 times the length of time we have." And in 1998, researchers at A&M University in Texas discovered that a chromosomal comparison between dolphins and humans showed an uncommonly close genetic makeup. Thirteen of 22 dolphin chromosomes were precisely identical with those of human chromosomes—a genetic similarity placing us closer in commonality than other land mammals, surprising University researchers who published their findings in *Cytogenetics and Cell Genetics* (the remaining nine dolphin chromosomes were mostly variations of their human counterparts). Is one-to-one interaction for both beings mere science fiction, or a real-life possibility?

Through additional research, I also learned the following dolphin facts:

- ❂ They are self-aware, able to recognize themselves in mirrored surfaces.

- ❂ They may be taught to recognize dozens of spoken words, and hundreds of hand-signals in countless combinations.

- ❂ They have successfully complied with language tasks more than any other creature.

- ❂ They have their own language with up to a *trillion* "words" possible.

But what struck me as most telling was this informational tidbit: "Dolphins have acute senses, which are faster and have a broader bandwidth than our [neuro-typical] senses...their sound interval discrimination ability is 10 times better than a human. Their acoustic system brings in data at something like 40 times our own rate at more than 10 times our frequency range." This fact corresponds with indigenously-autistic traits that, in turn, may relate to aligned, high-frequency vibration levels—portending unspoken, reciprocal interaction (remember the empathic attunement of my friends Colin and Carl, and Sean's animal encounters). Was this the essence for the connection between the ultra-high vibration of Adam's "plant-talk," Ashtyn's "animalspeak," and the voice of the dolphin?

Similar to at least half of all autistics, dolphins have also been shown to have elevated levels of serotonin, the "feel good" neurotransmitter that, consistent with the research of neuro-scientist Andrew Newberg and geneticist Dean Hamer, can impress our consciousness in mystical proportions. In an additional correlation, I discovered that dolphins are conscious breathers, meaning they are aware of taking every breath, not unlike the measured, meditative breathing necessary to achieve a spiritual plateau (which can cause serotonin to rise in humans). Moreover, if you keep current with paranormal research, we may wildly speculate that the high-frequency "chatter" of dolphins holds some parallel with identically-reported high-frequency Spirit "chatter" of the variety studied by the American Association of Electronic Voice Phenomena, a movement inaugurated by Thomas Edison in the 1920s.

By way of his definition, "communication is an exchange of information between two minds," Dr. John C. Lilly suggests that we must first acknowledge not only human-dolphin similarities in brain mass, but also in *minds*. According to his Interspecies Telepathic Project Website, dolphin researcher, Dr. Joe Champion, affirms the non-traditional communication potential between dolphins and humans:

> Numerous research attempts have been made since the mid-20th century to communicate with dolphins by training them to understand and speak human words. Even though minimal success has been achieved with this approach, results were greatly limited. This has been a major error in this field of dolphin communication, because dolphins do not possess the vocal ability necessary to

articulate the human language in a manner that would allow more comprehensive and interactive conversation.

Reports from telepathically-sensitive individuals in controlled situations in America and Russia, as well as from limited documented findings from U.S. Naval research, indicate a possible telepathic ability in dolphins. ["Program Plan for Anomalous Mental Phenomena" and "A Remote Action Investigation with Marine Animals" by Dr. Edwin May and Dr. Charles Pleass are two declassified Navy research documents involving dolphins and telepathy.] If one were to hypothesize that dolphins are telepathic, then it is through the "language" of telepathy that humans will be able to establish a more complete and interactive method of communication.

Telepathy aside, there is much to support an ongoing relationship between dolphin and autistic connections. The concept of dolphin therapy for children with disabilities (including autism) began in 1973 at the Seaquarium in Miami, Florida, under the guidance of linguist and acoustic phonetician, Dr. Hank Truby, who previously taught English to dolphins for 17 years. The effects of entrainment between dolphin and child vary, but often result in sustained play, increased attention span, and a peaceful calm. Most miraculous in the annals of such synergies includes "Tim," the Oldenburg, Germany, baby whom, in 1997, was aborted by his mother in her seventh month of pregnancy once she learned her fetus had Down syndrome. Though Tim was expelled moving and breathing, his heart beating fervently, the presiding physician did nothing to resuscitate him further, believing he would expire presently.

Yet 10 hours later, Tim still clung to life, and was finally treated—albeit with severe damage to his brain, lungs, and eyes, and, eventually, affects of autism. Adopted into a foster home the following year, Tim was exposed to dolphin therapy six years later, resulting in his improved digestion, motor skills, and speech.

The intuitive healing capacity of some dolphins to "target" the congenital abnormalities of others with sonar has been scientifically documented, a comparison made with medical ultrasound equipment. This exquisite degree of acoustic sensitivity in animals garnered international attention following the December 2004 tsunami that engulfed Sri Lanka and India coastlines, killing more than 150,000 people in a dozen countries, though very few animals were reported dead. Immediately preceding the devastating waves, eyewitnesses say elephants screamed and trampled for higher ground, dogs refused to be outdoors, flamingos deserted low-lying breeding areas, and zoo animals took shelter.

In keeping with the heart-brain entrainment studies conducted by the Institute of HeartMath, Australian researcher, Stephen Birch, author of *Dolphin-Human Interaction Effects*, showed that entrainment of the human EEG occurred during and after swims with free dolphins; that is, the human subjects' EEG reduced in frequency and increased in energy after swimming with free dolphins. Might this entrainment with dolphins lead to unlimited possibilities where autistic communication is concerned? It certainly seems plausible, and this very concept was affirmed for me by someone who knows both parties intimately.

Since 1988, Macy Jozsef has been the founder and director of Living From the Heart, a dolphin therapy retreat off the Florida coast and south-central Mexico that offers a six-day dolphin day camp for children with disabilities. Macy's investment in dolphin interaction is personal, as she explains why she established Living From the Heart. "In my journey to recover from breast cancer, I swam with dolphins, and for the first time since my diagnosis at age 30, I knew everything was going to be okay. The dolphins imparted that sense of total well-being to me, and I wanted to share that knowing with others." In facilitating swims with dolphins, Macy can validate "some of the magnificent changes we see when children with autism receive dolphin therapy. I have many, many past stories of positive changes, which occur when people participate in dolphin-assisted therapy."

Upon my initial inquiry about animal communication, Macy shared with me one story in particular. When I told her of my desire to unravel secrets the dolphins disclosed only to her autistic clients, Macy immediately related an anecdote that provided a satisfying summary to my investigation, and confirmed my intuitions about autistic-animal communication. Mike was a 5-year-old Mexican boy with autism who was introduced to Macy as someone not adequately wired for speech; he rarely spoke, and when he did it was with impulsive vocalization. "He *so* didn't talk," said Macy. "Almost like it wasn't in keeping with his personality."

After acquainting Mike with dolphin therapy, he took to it and seemed deliriously intoxicated with the experience. During his swim, Mike was euphoric—exhilarated and aglow with emotions untold—words were held captive by the neurological constraints that precluded his verbal expression. Macy was accustomed to witnessing similar reactions in countless other kids without speech. Both Macy and Andy, the dolphin trainer working with Macy in the water that day, sensed an epiphany awaken within the boy. Entranced in the moment, Andy ventured further, and tenderly asked, "What did the dolphin *say* to you, Mike?" In an emphatic burst of joy, and without hesitation, Mike blurted forth his spontaneous *spoken* reply, "Love!"

five

Ancestral Allies

"One sees clearly only with the heart. Anything essential is invisible to the eyes."

—*The Little Prince*

On Father's Day, June 18, 2006, I was gathered with some friends, a group of individuals who do not speak but, instead, type with varying degrees of physical support. On this particular day, we had a visiting author join us with a writing assignment for the group. The group was asked to compose their thoughts about someone meaningful in their lives.

Also joining us that Sunday afternoon was a newcomer, a teenage boy with autism named Aaron. He was accompanied to the gathering by his mother, father, and a staff support aide. It was an anxious time for Aaron: a new environment with foreign sights, sounds, and smells, and new friends who, while welcoming, required growing accustomed to. For the first hour, Aaron fidgeted, paced, and couldn't seem to relax or focus, understandably so. I offered to support him to type, but he seemed distracted.

Once the writing assignment was made, the family left with Aaron and moved into the quiet hallway outside our community center meeting room. I eventually joined them to ensure everything was alright and to reoffer my assistance to Aaron. By now, his anxiety had quelled enough to allow me to be present by his side, and we began the dance of communication, with me supporting his hand to type at his portable keyboard device.

As Aaron pecked out each individual letter, I gave sturdy, upward resistance as he pushed down against my hold to succinctly stroke the keypad. After each touch, I forcibly pulled his hand back to "clear the register" and give him time to motor-plan the next letter. Still mindful of the assignment, Aaron began to concentrate on the task at hand. Not surprisingly, he chose to write about his grandfather; but not just any grandfather, as the following transcript reveals:

Aaron:	I love my grandfather. He is forgiving.
Mother:	Maybe we should clarify which grandfather.
Aaron:	I love his blue eyes.
Stillman:	Is the grandfather with blue eyes in Spirit? Has he passed?
Mother:	Yes.
Stillman:	Then that's the one.
Father:	What is his name?
Aaron:	His name is love. He is helping others lern [sic] about love.
Stillman:	Do you still see him?
Aaron:	Y[es]. He is here today.

Aaron's mother explained that this particular grandfather had known Aaron only briefly as an infant before he passed. It was his father's father, and Aaron's dad confirmed that the grandfather had indeed passed on Father's Day—*observed that very Sunday*. The mother also said that when Aaron first began to type, he was forthcoming in sharing this kind of information about loved ones who had passed on.

During my experience with Aaron, no eerie lights flared nor did the chords of foreboding organ music cue, and Rod Serling did not emerge from the shadows to proffer his commentary. It *just happened*, simply and naturally and honestly. And yet, what might predispose some people on the autism spectrum to be privy to a mystical experience such as Aaron's and not others? There's nothing to support any of this in the autism research, save my own speculations on states of altered consciousness in *Autism and the God Connection*, in which I correspond autistic characteristics with cutting-edge spiritual science. For leads, I'd have to delve through studies stretching back to the 1940s—the very era during which Leo Kanner and Hans Asperger were engrossed in defining autism for the first time.

"Unusual Sensitivities in Very Young Children" is the paper contributed by Paul Bergman, MD and Sibylle K. Escalona, MD, and published in *Psychoanalytic Study of the Child*, 1949. Their findings collected observations of certain children, ranging in age from 3 months to 7 years old, who appeared to be sensory-defensive to environmental stimuli such as textures, temperatures, sounds, odors, and even colors. If you know autism intimately, you can accurately predict the consistent reactions of the studied children to such stimuli: they covered their eyes and ears, and rhythmically rocked their bodies to avert the hurtful assault on their nervous systems—precisely the self-regulation techniques commonly employed by autistics! Indeed, prior to its 1994 revision, the *Diagnostic and Statistical Manual of Mental Health Disorders* indicated such uncompromising sensory extremes as a distinguishing clinical trait of autism.

In my review of the parapsychology literature of this nature, it is curious that many other researchers describe autistic-like sensitivities without identifying subjects as autistic; and the acute degree of environmental-stress reaction first noted by Bergman and Escalona is referred to therein as *hyperesthesia*. In addition, I came upon a reference to another autistic experience called *synaesthesia*, when the borders of sensory function blur, overlap, and become cross-modal, causing an individual to, for example, "hear" colors, "smell" music, or "taste" shapes. These faculties are often linked to paranormal events, visions, and dreams. Further, Ernest Hartmann's *Boundaries of the Mind* coins two personality types via "thick" and "thin" boundaries: the latter group is open, vulnerable, and sensitive, with the autistic-like ability to immerse in an aspect of their lives—sometimes losing sense of time and space—in an experience known as *absorption*, which is also common to those with autism.

Most recently, Michael Jawer weaves such principles into his study "Environmental Sensitivity: Inquiry into a Possible Link with Apparitional Experience" published in the January 2006 *Journal of the Society for Psychical Research*. (Apparitional experience is herein defined as those experiences expanding beyond ordinary sensory perception, including precognition, telepathy, and a "general presence.") Jawer's questionnaire survey of adults included markers for those prone to "unusual sensitivity to light or sound" (a frequent indicator) as well as physical and mental health-related issues. Michael Jawer's conclusions draw many comparisons to the fragile way of being for many autistics that appear severely incapacitated. He states, "Persons who are extraordinarily sensitive *should* exhibit greater susceptibility" to ailments commonly associated with autism, such as allergies, chronic pain and fatigue, migraines, Irritable Bowel Syndrome, and possible electromagnetic influences. The majority of sensitive *males* who responded to the survey (remember that autism is four to five times greater in this gender) characterized themselves as "introverted or restrained," not unlike any number of men with Asperger's Syndrome.

As I explained to Aaron's parents that Father's Day, what Aaron had just communicated—his firsthand account of communions with his deceased grandfather—was very much in keeping with the reports shared with me by parents and caregivers from all over the country; there's no denying the very strong grandparent bond experienced by a number of autistic individuals who are so sensitively inclined. For those unfamiliar with this concept, the following several anecdotes are examples very typical of those relationships made known to me on a routine basis.

Mary, from northeastern Pennsylvania, says of her son Andrew's extrasensory perception:

Andrew's dad, Barry, has been doing family-tree research, and discovered that his great-great-grandfather
emigrated from Wales and fought in the Civil War. On
our way to the Outer Banks for our vacation, we decided to stop in Chancellorsville to check out one of
the battlefields where [the great-great-grandfather]
fought. While there, Barry and I commented how much
my father would have enjoyed learning about this family
connection to the Civil War because he was a Civil War
scholar. We then said maybe he was with us there in
Spirit. (My father died the year before Andrew was born.)
As we were leaving the battlefield, Andrew said, "Bye
George." My dad's name was George, and never do we
refer to him by his given name; just as "my/your dad" or,
"your grandfather." I guess he was there with us, and
Andrew knew it!

Julia's son, Adam, who has an affinity for plant life, also
has an attachment to pictures of deceased grandparents and
great-grandparents. Of this, Julia writes:

Some he has met, some he has not. These are the
only pictures that he takes an interest in, and carries
around periodically. Oddly enough, he will only carry
them around when it falls on the anniversary of their
death. This might seem odd, weird, or unsettling to some
people, but in my house it's pretty common.

I think my son is surrounded by a special light that
others see as well. I envy his view on the world. Do I feel
sorry for him? No. I feel sorry for the numerous parents
that I have come into contact with that can't see past

the label of "autism"; parents who are so stressed, they can only see their children for what they can't do and not what they can do. I feel that these children are here for a purpose, and only time will tell what that may be.

Debbi, from Ohio, shares that her father-in-Spirit once appeared to her in a nightly vision with foreknowledge of her future daughter's special needs:

> My father passed away when I was only 2 years old. I have no real memories of him; I had pictures, but no memories. Shortly after I was married, I was sleeping one night. I awoke and plain as day, standing at the foot of my bed, was the minister that had married my husband and me. We were married in Medina, Ohio (my husband's home town), and were currently living in Bolivar, which is close to Canton.
>
> The minister proceeded to tell me that my father needed to talk to me; that I needed to remember what he was saying to me as it would be very important one day. The next thing I knew, there stood my dad at the foot of my bed. It was so bizarre, as he was moving and talking. I remember thinking, "This is what my dad talks like." He told me many things: that he was sorry he had to leave me so soon; that he was proud of the person I had become; then he told me, "This is what you need to remember." He then stated, "We have a very special child chosen for you." He then continued, "This child will change your life, and make you very proud." He kept stressing how important it was for me to remember that.

I then woke up my husband and told him about it. I remember saying that it felt so real, like it was really him, but it couldn't be real because the minister that married us was still alive. So I decided it was just a very nice dream. The next day my husband was speaking to his parents in Medina. I noticed him become very quiet and turn a bit pale. He then hung up and told me that the minister who married us had passed away unexpectedly the day before, early in the day. To say we were shocked is an understatement.

A few years later, I became pregnant; no problems were expected, and all tests revealed a healthy baby. Then Elizabeth was born with Down syndrome as well as a multitude of health problems. It looked as if she would not make it; I just kept remembering my father's words and knew she would make it—and she did. Everything he said has come true. She has changed my life, and I am a much better person because of her. To say she has made us proud is an understatement, and boy, is she special. To this day, whenever we are in a tight spot with Elizabeth, I feel my dad's presence so strongly. I know he is her spiritual protector.

Claire, a Pennsylvania parent, and mom to 7-year-old son, Tommy, who has high-functioning autism, shares another common autistic occurrence:

Since Tommy was born, he always seemed to have someone "entertaining" him. I noticed that when he woke for feedings, he would stare up past me while I fed him, and would coo and smile at someone I couldn't see. After months of this, I finally asked my husband if he noticed it, and he said yes. Then he told me that the recliner we used to sit in to feed Tommy was in the exact spot that my deceased father-in-law would sit every evening to watch TV. I concluded then and there that Tommy's grandfather was watching over him.

One night when Tommy just would not go back to sleep, and continued to giggle and coo, I turned and looked over my shoulder to the spot where Tommy was looking, and said, "Alright Pap, Tommy needs to go to bed now," and Tommy promptly stopped his playing and drifted off to sleep. I was stunned and a little frightened. Later, when Trevor [another son on the autism spectrum] was an infant, he too played with his Pap. As they got older, they would sometimes seem to be talking to someone I couldn't see, in gibberish I couldn't understand. But there was definitely a "conversation."

Perpetual Planes of Learning

As you may have surmised from these samples, the overwhelming majority of incidents involving autistic capacity for interaction with deceased grandparents-in-Spirit almost always pertain to a grandfather, 66 percent by my calculation (from a random sample of three dozen reports). Interestingly, 53 percent of these spiritual connections come from a mother's side of the family—63 percent being reports of the mother's father or grandfather, and only 22 percent being the mother's mother or grandmother; likened with less than 30 percent from father's side, and a smattering where the genealogy was unknown to me because I hadn't thought it relevant to inquire. Even if grandfather and grandchild with autism never before met (because he passed before the child was born), the association is there, similarly evidenced by the autistic one preoccupied with the grandpa's picture, seemingly engaged in playful exchange with someone "invisible;" or drawing strength and perseverance from the grandpa's spiritual presence. By comparison, the protective presence of a grandmother-in-Spirit often takes on a maternal aspect, particularly tending to, coddling, and adoring the autistic toddler in the manner that Sabina's son perceives her deceased grandmother in the following example:

> He had been looking at a picture of my grandmother (and my namesake) and asked me, "Does your grandmother still send you pennies from Heaven?" My answer was "No, but she sends me blessings everyday." I was very taken by his question because, as a child, my grandmother would always send a birthday card and taped inside was a penny equal to my age at the time (five years=five pennies, and so on). I had never told my son about these cards until after he had asked his profound question. He, of course, informed me that he already knew that.

What was the purpose of this, I pondered, particularly where grandfathers were concerned? If we can accept that these relationships exist, what is their intention—comfort, love, security in an intolerant world? And is the relationship one-sided or two-sided? In other words, is the autistic individual

the exclusive recipient of whatever spiritual wisdom is imparted, or does the deceased grandfather benefit as well? I
began to wonder in these ways because of what I received
from Ursula, of New York, mom to teenage son Singen, who
has Asperger's Syndrome:

> A [very sensitive person] told me that my grandfa-
> ther was with Singen now; he has been helping Singen
> learn responsibility and independence, and Singen has
> been teaching my grandfather patience. She said I would
> see a great improvement in Singen through the year. Well,
> it's been another school year, and Singen has shown great
> improvement in his ability to get his homework com-
> pleted, and in taking care of himself. I told Singen that his
> great-grandpa Bradley was with him. I have to laugh be-
> cause my grandfather was not a very patient man, and it
> warms my heart to think that my son is teaching him
> patience.

It is fascinating to speculate that, even in Spirit, our loved
ones are imperfect and remain on a perpetual journey of spiritual education, such that the interactive relationship between
grandparent and autistic grandchild is *reciprocal*—a learning
opportunity, in varying degrees, for both parties. Could it be
that, in order to advance, grandparents-in-Spirit are required
to study the most basic themes of the autistic experience:
patience, tolerance, acceptance, sensitivity, and unconditional
love?

For further exploration of this theory, I interviewed my
dear friend Renee, a lovely young woman in her 30s with autism
and Down syndrome who lives in silence, but communicates

her true intellect through typing. (Renee has observed that "people don't appreciate the value of silence.") She relishes the irony of her deceiving exterior—which may be ignored or disregarded by others—that masks her keen intuition and unspoken knowledge. It is this foresight that enables Renee to perceive her place in the universe, granting temperance for adults similar to herself for whom recreational opportunities too often consist of Strawberry Shortcake puzzles, Little Golden Books, and *Lady and the Tramp* videos.

I yearned to speak with Renee because she had previously indicated to me that her mother's father, who had passed on, was "always available" to her. Renee was most gracious in accommodating my queries; her communication came hard and fast, and she seemed filled with an impassioned desire to convey her impressions to all. I began by asking her how it is that grandfathers appear most accessible to her and others. She replied:

> If a male is not a common male then he is usually accessible. My grandfather was a typical male who had manly hobbies like hunting, but the older he got the more gentle he became, and insightful always; just had to get a little older to lose the macho side. But he always was a man with open emotions.
>
> He is still learning from me. He says he watches closely but that's the other thing that goes with what I said; he was always a humble person, not too proud to listen and learn. I know he was always that way—even before I knew him. I've heard mom say that she was allowed to

disagree with him, and did, and it didn't make him angry
like that sort of thing made my dad's dad angry.

I next asked Renee what her grandfather is continuing to
learn from her, if anything, even in his transformed state. She
replied:

> That I can communicate with him in a way he only
> glimpsed when he was alive on Earth. He knows I per-
> ceive things he never realized even though I facilitated
> [communication] a few years before he died. He knows
> how I feel before I perceive myself telling him, and I look
> to him for strength in a way he never before knew I did;
> but he was too humble to see his effect on me until the
> clutter of this world was cleared away. Now he says it's
> the kind of thing that's crystal clear.

Renee's semantics connote Singen's grandfatherly tutor-
ship, as well as Aaron's observation that his deceased grandfather is "forgiving," among others. The conclusion being
contended is that some men—headstrong, even obstinate,
"man's man" males—who mellowed later in life, were also can-
didates for a unique, intentional, and reciprocal relationship
with their autistic grandchildren. (This contention is made all
the more curious in contrast to my previous speculation that
one purpose served by autism is a tempering of the male gender.) In reverse, the sublime implications were stunning: if some
autistics could align in synchronous entrainment with plants,
animals, and human beings, still others were also capable of
the same divine synchrony with loved ones (grandfathers)-in-
Spirit; a real-time, one-on-one glorious manifestation of love,

harmonious and pure—each learning from one another. It was a mind-boggling prospect.

By extension, this philosophy begged a dark inquiry: if our very sensitive loved ones on the autism spectrum perceive and interact with divine entities, including grandparents-in-Spirit, might they be as equally open in perceiving low-energy apparitions of ill intent?

six

Nosmo the Nefarious

"By heaven, I'll make a ghost of him that lets me!"

—Hamlet

I f ever I had any reservations about including the "Ghosts in the Laboratory" chapter in *Autism and the God Connection*, those feelings were completely assuaged about seven months prior to that book's publication when I learned of a situation that was nearly identical, but far more intense. "Ghosts in the Laboratory" relates the experiences of Josh, a young man with autism, who was so sensitive that he was perceiving a number of intrusive entities that were infiltrating his home—and his consciousness. The phantoms were originating from a disheveled cemetery located on a far corner of the property where Josh had recently moved; when he communicated specific names of the spectres, his support staff was able to identify them as those on the ancient 1800s-era headstones.

When taking a break during a consultation for another client, I confided some of what was in my then-forthcoming book with Barb, the client's case manager, with whom I enjoyed a sound rapport, and Rhonda, the agency coordinator, with whom I had also collaborated on previous cases. When I shared a bit about Josh's story, it immediately struck a chord with both women, and they began to tell bits and pieces about Victor, a middle-aged man with autism who had a long history—and severe reputation—for very difficult-to-manage "multiple-personality-type" behaviors. Vic, they told me, had once lived in a local Victorian, described as a "dump" prior to renovations that made it habitable as a group home for five people with mental retardation. It was common knowledge that the place was haunted; it was "certified" as just that by a paranormal society that had investigated the complaints of previous owners. Legends and rumors stretched back 25 years or more, and the house was the subject of Halloween radio broadcasts and pastoral blessings. Though he no longer lived there, Vic was reportedly plagued by "presences" about which he talked while at the house. The situation had gone unchecked to a degree that Vic's own personality was blurred when he routinely became "host" to several personalities. At times he would insist, "Don't call me Vic, call me (one of his pseudonyms)." Neither anti-psychotic medications nor psychiatric hospitalizations alleviated his condition, which he had endured *for more than 20 years*!

When I mentioned the potential for me to counsel Victor's support staff, Barb and Rhonda were eager to have me back, but the great driving distance from my home would require coordinating the trip with other work in the area, and that would have to wait about six months. Still, I was anxious for additional clues of whatever details they could fill in. Closer to my impending trek to Vic's territory that spring, I rang up Barb, left a voice-mail message requesting the information, and awaited her return response.

Within a couple days, Barb called me with the kind of details I was seeking. While living in the house, Vic—and others—perceived a little girl, Katie, who came to "visit," and who was observed looking out toward the front of the house. Staff workers would regularly discover a single dead bird in the attic, sometimes on a daily basis. And the enormous mirror mounted above the fireplace—an ominous centerpiece that dominated the first floor—was the focus of unsettling activity, so much so, that, in time, it was covered over with a blanket to avert any further distractions. Barb also listed some of the known personalities Vic manifested. There was Katie, the little girl. Vic was also "Sissy," but she was thought to be transient and had dissipated. When his mother used to call Vic, he would say he was *her* or "Pooh." Sometimes when Vic committed acts of self-injury, he was "Lib" or Baby Albert.

"Oh, there's also Nozzmoeking," Barb told me.

"Nozzmoeking?" I asked. "Can you spell it?"

"It's N-O-S-M-O K-I-N-G," she explained, "Like *NO SMOKING.* I think it was a local TV character years ago."

The name was a clever anagram, one that would require some research. Apparently when Vic was at his worst, he assumed this *nom de plume* as his own. In the days to follow, Nosmo King would unexpectedly trespass my thoughts with disturbing frequency, usually when my mind was reposed. What did it mean, I wondered.

In the interim, Jackie, Vic's present case manager, had mailed some photocopies of newspaper articles dating to 1981. The stories documented goings-on that were more spectacular than I had imagined, and interviewed in-depth the Abbott Samuels family, current owners of the house. Jackie told me that between their residency and Vic's stay, there had been other families that came and went. An undated clipping told of the house's approval by a zoning board for use as a community group home for $450 monthly rent to its landlord who salvaged it. "It's just a nice, old Victorian house. And I don't like to see these kinds of homes destroyed," the man was quoted as saying. He also went on record as dismissing any gossip of hauntings. "I'm sure there's no ghosts there. I put in new wiring and plumbing. And I broke almost every wall in the place. And I haven't seen one ghost."

It all sounded unbelievably suspicious; the sort of sordid tale that tends to take on a life of its own, a prank perpetrated by bored teens and thrill-seekers—just the kind of autumnal punch to perk local media from a lackluster slump. And there was Vic—at age 41, his reputation preceded him as a confused, out-of-control man who sometimes vacillated a fine line between himself and decidedly feminine personas (he had even tucked his penis between his legs, providing the illusion of female genitalia). Wasn't it possible that Vic did, in fact, experience a legitimate mental health issue that caused him to think himself into another character? It sounded like "grandiosity," one symptom of mania—the Richter-scale portion of bipolar disorder—in which someone believes themselves to be omnipotent and superhuman. In children and people with limited life experience (such as those with autism or mental retardation), I have seen individuals refer to themselves as the Easter Bunny...Batman...Elvis...God. Rarer still, but a definite possibility, was a true personality disorder. On the other hand, it was conceivable that if Vic were engaged in an authentic battle for control with an opposing menace—real or hallucinated (which would *seem* real to him regardless)—his mental health *would* erode through time. Wouldn't yours? What to make of it…. Enter the nagging Mr. Nosmo King.

Finding Nosmo

As a preface, let's remember that we're talking about a person on the autism spectrum. As I cautioned those readers of Josh's story in *Autism and the God Connection*, please know that so many people with autism construe what they perceive in ways that are very direct, literal, and concrete. They say what they mean, and mean what they say. Let's also remember that if you are seen as mentally retarded—a perpetual child who is rarely treated as an adult—your life experiences are limited to what's provided to you; you can only know what you know. In so doing, you use as a point of reference that which is within the purview of your life experience, even by way of comparisons or analogies. If people are unpresuming of your intellect, and believe you possess juvenile aptitude, that's how they'll interface with you. That's how they'll know what to get you for holidays and birthdays, and that's what they'll play when they sit you in front of a television—kid stuff.

Readers may also recollect from *Autism and the God Connection* my lengthy discussion on decoding autistic hieroglyphics—symbolic iconography that comes through in similes and metaphoric communications. One typical instance is that of the 29-year-old man with autism who didn't speak but—

since he was a toddler—possessed an inexplicable passion for
United States presidents. Not just any presidents, though; he
was fascinated with those prominent on Mount Rushmore,
and, in particular, he was drawn to Abraham Lincoln. This is
logical when the passion's *symbolism* is deciphered: the young
man identified with Lincoln's persistence in the face of ad-
versity, his clemency for the fair and equable treatment of
those oppressed, and his purity of motive in emancipating a
subjugated people. His example is indicative of the communication indigenous to those who abide mainly in silence.

The Internet is a wonderful resource at one's fingertips,
and that's where I began my search on Vic's behalf. I entered
"NOSMO KING," and perused the findings: a Lubbock, Texas,
band formed in the summer of 2002—too recent; the stage name
of Vernon Watson who toured U.K. music halls prior to and
after WWI, and who passed away in 1949—before Vic's time. I
wasn't coming upon anything relevant. Then I remembered
Barb saying that Nosmo King was an area TV character on a
long-defunct children's program. I typed in "NOSMO KING
TV" and made a curious discovery.

Adventuretime was a fondly recalled kiddie show hosted
daily by Paul Shannon on Pittsburgh's WTAE-TV, Channel 4,
from 1959 to 1975. Shannon revived the career of the Three
Stooges after they appeared on his show, and played Kimba
the Lion cartoons, among others. Most significantly, I learned
Shannon also sometimes appeared as his sinister alter-ego,
Nosmo King, a character who "stalked about the studio in a
slouch hat and overcoat, and who never spoke." Now the stray
jigsaw fragments began to assemble: a sinister alter-ego who

never spoke, lurked in the shadows cloaked in disguise, and conveyed a foreboding presence to all. If I grew up occupied by *Adventuretime*, retained readily-playable mind-movies of such memories, as so many autistics are capable of, *and* needed a way to communicate my *adult* impressions of an intrusive, diabolical entity—that I couldn't articulate in a more *adult* way—wouldn't Nosmo King make the perfect patsy? It fit, but required fleshing out.

I needed more information about the house's history from its 1800s construction and original tenants through present day, or at least through Vic's tenure. One of the news articles Jackie had sent interviewed Abbott Samuel III and his wife.

Another Internet search provided Mr. Samuel's name, address, and telephone number, and I promptly placed a call. "Mr. Samuel, my name is William Stillman. I'm calling from the Hershey area. I'm a consultant who specializes in helping people to understand autism in children and adults, and I'm going to be consulting for a man who once lived in the same house as you did." When I mentioned the address and location of the house, Mr. Samuel indicated that he never lived there.

"I'm trying to help this man because I know that the house is said to be haunted."

"Wasn't me," he said.

"Well, are there other Abbott Samuels that you know of?"

"Yeah, there's a few."

"Mr. Abbott Samuel III?" I asked.

"Yes," he countered.

> "Well, sir, I'm looking at a picture of you in a clipping
> from the *Times-Ledger* dated 1981, and it says Abbott
> Samuel III."
>
> "I never lived there. You got the wrong guy."

Click. He hung up, end of conversation. Maybe I struck a
nerve, trolling for unpleasant reminiscences of a quarter-century
past; or maybe I *did* have the wrong guy, but then how many
Abbott Samuel III in that vicinity could there be? I had encountered my first obstacle. Strike two was that the Roman
Catholic pastor, quoted in one of the news articles as being
without an explanation for the eerie events, had passed away
in 1998. Even the monsignor of the presiding dioceses wasn't
able to offer any background, though he did express concern
over Vic's apparent loss of free will ("Is this a case of posses-
sion?" he had asked). The retired radio celebrity, who had
once covered the story on two consecutive Halloweens, never
returned my call. The paranormal investigator originally involved was nowhere to be found, but was allegedly still alive
and well. And the county historical society was of no help
either, suggesting I apply for a deed to obtain the home's lin-
eage (though Barb thought she could pull a few strings with a
contact at the county courthouse). It seemed that anyone who
had a connection to the mysterious residence wasn't talking,
couldn't talk, or would just as soon forget. I was on my own.

My strategy for counseling Vic's support staff was sev-
eral-fold. First, it was imperative that they reenvision Vic
through an alternate prism; this required shattering myths
and stereotypes about autism and "behaviors" long attributed
to Vic's way of being. In order to best serve him, they were

obliged to accept what he was telling them as the truth; regardless of their own personal beliefs, it was still *his* truth and this was to be honored. (Imagine trying to communicate to those around you terrifying circumstances and events that were ignored, written off, and chalked up to your being "crazy"; and your relief to at long-last be believed.)

Second, I needed a better sense of Vic's mental stability; how might his struggle have manifested in anxiety, depression, post-traumatic stress disorder, or even bipolar disorder—the most common mental health issues I've encountered in persons with autism. I was told that Vic had an abusive childhood: an embittered, indifferent mother; a stern and stoic ex-military step-father; and bouts with bizarre treatments such as dangling Vic upside down from a backyard clothesline, effecting a sanguine rush to replenish the orifices of a brain compromised. This knowledge would aid me in separating the wheat from the chaff in determining what was real and what was symptomatic of mental health manifestations. This many years into it, the two were likely inextricably intertwined; reputed discarnate entities are essentially parasitic "bottom-feeders." They thrive upon the self-loathing, depleted self-esteem, malaise, anxiety, addictions, and aftereffects of abuse in those most vulnerable, such as Vic. In him, they had found the perfect victim: someone deficient of confidence and esteem, someone who had all but surrendered to self-deprecation. If they fed from higher-energy sensations, they would've moved on and transitioned to the Heavenly realm long ago. Their very sustenance relied upon sustaining Vic's suffering, and Vic's suffering nourished them—the proverbial vicious cycle. Author Joseph Chilton

Pearce discusses the sorrowful toll shame can effect when one stands so accused, abused, and marginalized as Vic had been. "Shamed in this sense, we forget who we are. We actually become the protective mask we adopt to shield us from the accusing fingers pointed toward us. Cut off from our spirits, we spend the rest of our life trying to prove our innocence." So far as I was concerned, Vic's innocence had been irretrievably violated years ago. Wary of this, an important aspect of my proposed intervention for Vic was motivated by the premise of Cognitive-Behavior Therapy, basically helping Vic to replace negative thoughts and feelings with positive, healing ones—a challenging undertaking for one so deeply entrenched in the murky bog of abhorrence.

Finally, I wanted to tap the spirituality of those around Vic who were open to prayer and meditation if they were willing to include Vic in their times of solace.

The three-hour trip to meet Vic and his team felt "off." Minor hindrances seemed contrived to delay me en route. Barb came to pick me up at the hotel to escort me the 45 additional minutes to our respective meeting place. When I got in, she handed me a packet of questionnaires that Vic's past and present staff had filled out about his different names and alternate personas.

In addition to those of which I was already aware, there were others. Some had logical explanation: "Lib" derived from Liberace, the object of his mother's adulation; so much so, that, in order to capture her sporadic attention, the young Vic would call himself Liberace. Frank Sinatra and "Boogie Bear" also seemed to have their roots in pop culture. Shit-for-Brains, the name Vic used to berate himself, was clearly an epithet with which he had once been degraded. Others were ambiguous, such as No-Name, who often emerged with Nosmo King. Sometimes, two "personalities" would conflict, like a battle of words between No-Name and Liberace, instigated by No-Name. In the past, Vic had sobbed uncontrollably in duress that "they" were fighting with him; swore "I'll kill them all" while punching walls; and repeated over and over, "I'm going to hit No-Name." Spates of self-aggression were not uncommon, and Rhonda told me that Vic would slap his own face, but reverse the position of his hand so that he reddened his flesh as though his open palm was that of another. At the height of distress, Vic had pleaded, "I need help, please help me...he's mean to me...keep an eye on him."

Confrontation

Upon our arrival at Barb and Jackie's office, Vic's staff began filing into our meeting room. Barb intended to transcribe our dialogue on her laptop computer, which she would project onto the wall for all to see. But when she assembled it on the projector, only the computer desktop image projected; the laptop screen remained totally blank—a first for this device, Barb confessed.

Soon, Vic walked in and was introduced to me. When I facilitate the consultation process for teams supporting individuals, I always go in "cold." That is, I never ask for any background information in advance. I've found that so often—especially in instances where someone is challenging to support—their history of "behaviors" can color my perception to the point of being unduly influenced. However, this instance was different; I had deliberately requested as much background information as possible. But Vic was far more lucid than what I was expecting, given my review of past violent incidents. His demeanor was calm and composed; he couldn't have been more cooperative and accommodating— an affect that drew suspicion from a few who knew him well. His face was pale and unblemished, his eyes clear and blue— an open canvas made more expansive by his shaved crown. His slightly startled expression conveyed a sense of boyish wonder.

Before introductions, Vic seated himself next to Barb at her request. She was gracious in ensuring that he would be po- sitioned to a full view of the projected laptop on the wall, and within proximity to be heard by her to accurately capture his contributions. I began the meeting by explaining why I was present, and that I desired to be of service to Vic. I quickly allayed his chief concern: being unwillfully committed to psy- chiatric hospitalization. I affirmed that was not my intent; I merely wished to gather information in order to craft a blue- print to aid him. Once assured, it was *Vic* who broached the sub- ject of ghosts, taking me by surprise with his ready offer so early in the discussion. I followed his lead, gently allowing him to guide the conversation and asking questions only as I saw fit.

Vic said that there were just two primary presences, Baby Albert and Sissy. Baby Albert was a man of about 30, but his name was a misnomer as Vic expressed, "Yes, what he would say, 'Baby would cry.' There was a baby—in your heart, inside— you could hear her cry." Sissy was 20, said Vic, with long, brown hair; she still visited him in his new location and, indeed, Vic once came downstairs with a blanket bundled to look like a swaddled infant—Sissy's baby, he alleged. Not wanting to dwell too long on the subject of ghosts, I asked to table the discussion and come back to it later. Vic agreed.

I next led the team through a framework for bipolar symptoms developed by Dr. Robert Sovner, the late psychiatrist with a special interest in the mental health issues of persons with developmental disabilities. Psychiatry is not an exact science. Far from it, psychiatry was once described to me by one clinician as "a crap shoot," that is, guess-work, albeit *educated* guesswork. But one need not be a PhD or an MD to discern mental health symptomology; in fact, psychiatrists rely upon our ability to do so, especially in the development disabilities field in which clients are usually seen quarterly for, on average, 15 minutes at a time. Any psychiatrist in this position, particularly one challenged in sorting through autism and mental illness, would be vulnerable to the information exchanged from a caregiver, which is oftentimes subjective, emotional descriptions of aggressive client "behaviors," not *symptoms*. Our responsibility as caregivers is one of education to planfully prepare for an informed dialogue with the presiding psychiatrist about symptomology, not pathology.

For Vic, the symptoms of depression were uncertain; only portions seemed to apply; the symptoms of mania held better context, but still didn't paint a finished portrait. Of greatest conflict was some ambiguity for grandiosity, perhaps the most distinguishing element of the illness.

In grandiosity, there is a sense of inflated self-esteem far beyond the reaches of what it typical. Grandiose individuals may believe themselves all-powerful, possessing of unearthly strength (which can be demonstrated by trashing their living arrangement: flipping sofas, sending televisions airborne, punching out windows). They may refer to themselves as larger-than-life characters, and exert demanding, controlling influence over others. Manifesting authoritarian "names" by which an individual insists they be addressed could certainly be an aspect, but this didn't seem so for Vic. He wasn't employing Baby Albert, No-Name, Liberace, or even Nosmo King to lord and command over his support staff; they were just *there*, and it was unclear if they even surfaced in conjunction with other manic symptoms.

Vic was holding up beautifully despite a very delicate discussion. We all took a much-needed break before reconvening.

I next introduced the concept of being inherently gentle and exquisitely sensitive, as so many with autism can be; attuned to all things seen and unseen as it relates to the senses being magnified above what is usual. I explained that "ghosts" were different from Spirits of loved ones in Heaven. A loving presence will only ever be a loving presence, I pledged; a loving presence would never be intrusive, create anxiety and chaos, or cause someone to use another name. Conversely, ghosts are "stuck" and can attach, similar to a magnet, onto others most vulnerable.

Now when I revisited the subject, Vic's attitude shifted and he became defensive and evasive, attempting to change the subject.

> "Vic, is there a time when you want Albert and Sissy to stop visiting you?"

"Yeah."

"Would you prefer they left you alone?"

"Yes."

"What does Sissy say to you?"

"She is in the house now. I love the mini-mart. Sissy is a friend of Vic, but wants her to let him alone."

"They can be selfish..."

"That's right."

"...because they don't see Heaven."

"Bill, what did you have for supper last night?"

"A bowl of Grape-Nuts. Do you understand, Vic?"

"Do you eat grapes? How do you spell elephant?"

"I'd prefer to continue our conversation, if you don't mind."

"What did you have for supper last night?"

"I already told you that, Vic. You can tell them no...you can get some sleep at night."

"I want to be a gentleman...no baby, no Sissy."

"You can tell them to go away."

"I am good today...I like that word, 'you are good.'"

"*They are like bottom-feeders, Vic.*"

At this, Vic glowered, shot me a defiant glance, and rasped under his breath, "*Nosmo King.*" I had pressed one button too many, so I acquiesced.

Barb continued typing the transcript as the words appeared, pecked out on the wall, one by one. Just then, something strange

happened. As soon as Barb had completed my recommenda-
tion about the power of prayer, the sentence suddenly deleted
itself—without viable explanation—and she was obliged to re-
type that portion back into the document.

I conjectured that the greatest challenge to conquer and
defeat unwanted solicitations—to effect Vic's victory—lay
within Vic himself. When I asked the team who loves Vic, I
was met with disconcerting silence. *The meeting group knew of
no one who loved him.* No harmonious patterns, no entrainment with either man *or* beast here. Vic had been disillusioned,
abandoned, or betrayed by anyone in a position to give him what
he wanted and needed most. How easily seduced he must've been
by the presence of those discarnate souls who promised him fulfillment. Overcoming required that Vic learn to love, not loath,
himself. It was an attribute absent and a strength unrealized,
but a requirement for warfare nonetheless.

Preventative Measures

Once Vic's staff felt comfortable with my consultations, they
began to open up more and more, inviting me to visit Vic's
present house, shared with three other men, and relating unusual experiences of their own. Vic's new home had been 1800s-
era slave quarters adjacent to an historic mansion, razed long
ago (a parking lot overrun with weeds was in its stead); the
side street, on which the house shared an address, wasn't
macadamed with black-top but remained intact, paved with
ancient yellow brick—once a common building material in that
area (a *real* yellow brick road, I mused). It was reported to
me that, when alone in the place, staff felt the unease of being

watched; one female staff person swore she heard footsteps walk across the kitchen floor, and it was not uncommon for staff on the overnight shift to discover that, invariably, the front- and back-locked doors had unlocked themselves come morning. I, myself, had overheard Vic having a two-way argument in the bathroom with a slightly-deeper-voiced male (Nosmo?). And I had observed Vic throttle himself by grabbing hold of his shirt collar (again, in reverse as if someone stood before him), and berating himself with, "Better not say that again, buddy boy!" No matter Vic's anguished impetus, be it a combination of mental health and otherworldly symptoms, there was still an internal turmoil ever-brewing just below the surface, always threatening to boil over at a moment's notice.

Part-antidote, part-balm to salve decades of psychological wounds, I composed a story for Vic to reinforce his positive traits and diminish his self-loathing, replacing negative thinking with good thoughts. It was suggested that Vic's staff read the story with him before bedtime. At first he resisted the addition, but shortly he took to it, and, soon, actually looked forward to reading the story. Most importantly, Vic began to transfer the story's concepts to circumstances beyond the nightly ritual—which is just as I had hoped—by stating, "I'm a good person" after completing a successful or altruistic act. Vic's staff was also advised to watch for "teachable moments," opportunities to catch him doing something good and praise him for it, thus underscoring the story's tenets. My theory was that if within Vic there existed less and less negative emotion, he'd be less attractive for any would-be apparition attachments. Here is Vic's story:

> I am a good person.
>
> Some of the ways that I am a good person include
>
> _____ .
>
> There are things about my life that are good and happy.
>
> There are things about my life that were sad and upsetting.
>
> The things that were sad and upsetting *are not my fault.*
>
> I will try not to think about things that make me sad or upset.
>
> Because I am a good person, I will try to think good things about myself.
>
> If I forget to do this:
>
>   ◉ I will try to remember that I am a good person.
>
>   ◉ My staff will remind me that I am a good person.
>
>   ◉ I can talk about all the ways that I am a good person.
>
> I will try to stay safe from harm.
>
> I will do my best to try to stay calm and not harm anyone if I am feeling upset.
>
> I will try to remember that I am a good person.

Vic was also one to personally internalize the loss of any staff person who left him (group homes in the community can have notoriously high turn-over rates). To ensure he understood any perceived abandonment was not his fault, we implemented another story to that end:

> There are people in my life who come and go.
>
> Sometimes I wish some people would stay longer.
>
> When people leave me, it may be because:
>
> ⚙ They got a new job.
>
> ⚙ They moved away.
>
> ⚙ They don't have as much time to spend with me as they used to.
>
> It may be for other reasons.
>
> This happens to everyone.
>
> When people leave me, it is not my fault.
>
> When some people leave me, I may miss them and feel unhappy.
>
> It natural to feel unhappy, and that is okay.
>
> When people leave me, I will try to remember that they have reasons.
>
> When people leave me, I will try to remember that I am a good person, and it is not my fault.

Vic's team and I continued intensive discussions about bipolar symptoms, and they became increasingly aware that Vic may have been cycling through *both* mania and depression at least once daily. Vic's psychiatrist was appreciative of the renewed attention to detail in order to better serve Vic, such that a lessening of bipolar symptoms, despite the constancy of his "haunting," validated the legitimacy of that experience. Whenever Vic would cite a name other than his own, his staff was consistent in communicating, "Tell him/her to get out," to which Vic gradually complied. Slowly, a new personality crept in, gaining resilience with each passing day: Vic, alone and by himself.

Vic's healing had begun, but it was very much a process that would take time. We were attempting to undo many years of destructive, "learned" behaviors brought about by physical and mental abuse in addition to an apparent psychological invasion by phantom forces—a new psychiatric paradigm to heed. Therein lies my plea for a modern, revisionist discipline that acknowledges, in circumstances similar to Vic's, all three of the following bear true for the individual so compromised: autism, mental illness, and entity sabotage. (It would not be the last time I'd be conferred upon under such conditions.) Sifting through these components will require our adopting progressive paradigms combined with the best of science and humanistic techniques.

Vic's mood and attitude stabilized and, in addition, I recommended that the house be blessed for good measure. There was still occasional friction with his three housemates—such is the limitation of the group home system—and Vic still contended with bipolar disorder; however when last I saw him, Vic asked me to comfort him by tenderly taking his hand in mine. His anxiety pacified for the moment, Vic hugged me good-bye as I departed the house and stepped out onto the yellow brick road just beyond his front porch.

PART III

Higher
Ground

seven

Prince of Peace

*"Where there is great love there are always
miracles."*

—Willa Cather

Of all the relationships in our lives that matter most,
perhaps none is more personal and private than the one
we share with the Source of our Creation, regardless of the
creed by which we honor that Source. Because their lives have
not yet begun, children are often considerably closer to the
Source than most adults. But in pursuing autism and a God
connection, I've noticed a new trend emerging in the responses
I receive to my research, one that, initially, took me unaware.
Here's an example from Marty, dad to young Matt:

> We stopped at the National Shrine at Mount St. Mary's
> in Emmittsburg, Maryland about a year after our son Matt
> was diagnosed with moderate autism, six years ago at age
> 3. He had begun to regain some speech, but was still
> quite echolalic in his patterns. Well, he was perseverating
> on Batman action figures at the time, and left one at the

base of the statue for Mary, "For her to give to Jesus." Of course, my wife, Barbara, and I were moved at his action, and from that point forward we saw marked improvement in Matt. Yes, he was receiving lots of treatment and therapy, but we both believe that it was divine intervention that helped in his recovery.

What interested me about Marty's story wasn't Matt's "marked improvement" so much as Matt's cognizance of Jesus—the recipient of Matt's unselfish offering. Those of you who know autism intimately understand how all-absorbing someone's passion can be, in this example Matt's strong fondness for Batman; that Matt selflessly donated one of his prized possessions "to give to Jesus" is out of character and out of the ordinary. Clearly something extraordinary moved Matt to enact this loving gesture.

Curiously, I was hearing more and more about such autistic encounters with Jesus or a Christ-like figure, such as that of Sabina from southeast Missouri, who wrote, "My son continues to amaze me with his insights. During a recent conversation, he could not understand why I am unable to remember being with him, other family members, and Jesus in Heaven. He says it was the best place he has ever been and likes to think about it a lot. I wish I could remember, and I hope he never loses the ability to have these memories."

At first, the influx was a bit disconcerting—what about those families who are non-denominational, or those of Hebrew faith? Then I remembered, Jesus *was* a Jew; He was adoring of all children regardless of race or heritage (or disability for that matter), so I respectfully deduced that visions of Him have less to do with Christianity, and more to do with conveying His message of unconditional love. I was pleased to find my intuition validated by the leading researcher of these experiences.

In his book, *I Am with You Always: True Stories of Encounters with Jesus*, G. Scott Sparrow, psychotherapist and assistant professor at the University of Texas-Pan American, catalogues and categorizes such modern-day visions for the first time, and qualifies similar experiences among the neurotypical population by stating, "As many of the recipients of these experiences have discovered, one does not have to believe any particular thing about Christ in order to find him deeply involved in our most life-changing experiences."

Dr. Sparrow has also collected encounters of those who are non-Christian with a mystical or Christ-like being, including that of a Jewish woman who actively practices Judaism, but is open to all religions and the unity of all people. Her experience led her to magnanimously conclude, "...that Jesus is pure love and God is that pure love, and we are all meant to grow to be that pure love and become one with all creation." In another instance, a woman's meditation was interceded by a Light Being, a spiritual presence that pulsated. When she asked, "Who are you?" the Being replied, "Some call me Buddha, some call me Christ." When the woman indicated that she didn't "know" Buddha, the Being answered, "Then I am Christ."

Given all that we've discovered about the dichotomy of consciousness—the autistic capacity to sometimes "slip the surly bonds of Earth"—and the practice of entrainment, might it be that those perceived as meek, disabled, or severely impaired are *more* likely predisposed to such manifestation? This is the premise of my book, *Autism and the God Connection*, in which I document autistic communions with high-vibration entities, ascribed as angels by some, from which the individual receives respite, humor, rejuvenation, and love. One of Dr. Sparrow's neuro-typical subjects emerged from her spontaneous Christ encounter in a manner that echoes these findings: "Increasingly, I walked a narrower path, with a knowing which surmounted logical reasoning. Trust increased. Discernment became clearer. Barriers melted. Surprises came. Meditation became more frequent. And I realized that being in communion with Him means manifesting His love in fuller ways with others, as well as with myself, than I'd known before."

And so it would seem a number of autistics appear to have a deeply personal relationship with Jesus—an exalted antithesis to the damaging disharmony of someone such as Vic. In compiling this chapter, I had all but disregarded my own empathic encounter as a 6 year old—grieving with abandon, beholding a stained-glass window of the crucifixion—until I read the following story submitted by Cherie from Newark, New Jersey, a story virtually identical to my own:

> Domenick, age 5 now, was diagnosed with PDD-NOS [an experience on the autism spectrum] at age 2-and-a-half, so it's been a long period that I have coped with getting him needed treatment and assistance. As always described in your book, Domenick has had a spiritual quality; his first memorized words were the Hail Mary, and he kisses the cross wherever we go—he is evidence of God's existence to all of us on a daily basis.

Last month, my family and I took Domenick to a new church that has a beautiful mural of Jesus crucified on the ceiling near the altar. We sat in a front pew and did not really notice it. Within minutes, Domenick lay on his back in the pew and began to sob uncontrollably, pointing at the image of Christ crucified. He did not stop until we left at the end of Mass. He appeared to be weeping with sorrow. We were all dumbfounded.

Might the Christian prophecy of resurrection come not as One, but as One fused in Spirit and embodied by the works of many? Cherie's background as mother to a child with a different way of being, and her desire to find spiritual fulfillment unique to her circumstances, led her to found a successful New Jersey support group for parents called And a Child Shall Lead Us. Likewise, Lisa's son, Talyor, seems to perpetuate the ideal of One personified through many:

From the time he was a baby he would look to a spot in the air and laugh. Later at about 3 years old, he started talking about Jesus (we never even went to church, he was never around talk of Jesus or God). He would talk with Jesus and see "angels" all the time. He's now age 9, but just last summer he asked, "Do you *really* not see the angels?" Last year he told me how sad he was for me that I never saw Jesus or talked to him. He lays his hand on us (anyone in our family) when we are hurt and prays for us. He has always said things that have blown me away and I am left thinking, "If he doesn't talk to Jesus, how does he know these things?" Once when I was stressed out, he put his palm on my cheek and said, "Shhh...be quiet and let Jesus fill the air."

Animals adore him, butterflies land on him all the time; cats and dogs treat him like a king. We had a cat that was aloof with everyone else, but would actually *guard* Taylor—like a guard dog—standing in front of Taylor, and hissing at the supposed threat. Everywhere we go, people fall in love instantly with him—it's weird. People ask for pictures of him, tell me how special he is, ask if he's up for adoption (thankfully they laugh when they ask those kinds of questions). I think he just may have an aura surrounding him that draws people and animals.

He used to say he wished he could go live with Jesus and would ask when he could die so he could go live with Jesus. It really scared me, but he would wistfully say, "Jesus is just so good Mommy, it'd be so great to be with him all the time." Thankfully I got him to quit saying that by telling him that Jesus put him here on Earth for a reason, and 80 years or so on Earth would be nothing compared to eternity. He tilted his head and said, "Yeah, I know (sigh). I have to make everyone understand the physics of life." I was so startled that he had even *said* the word *physics*, I didn't react for a minute; then when I finally asked him about what he meant, he said, "I didn't mean to say that, I meant something else," and would not say any more about it.

Taylor was born 15 weeks premature, and twice they told me he would not make it through the night. He was diagnosed with PDD-NOS, ADHD, SID, Apraxia of Speech, and Tourette's syndrome. I thank God for every second that he is with me. Our family has definitely become more spiritual since Taylor. After knowing Taylor, you just know that God and Jesus exist and are real.

Taylor does get sad sometimes that he hasn't seen God. He was trying to "help" me see angels a few weeks ago, pointing out where they were, and pointed to the middle of his forehead and said, "You have to see from here, Mom." I'm so thankful to you just to know that there are other kids out there like Taylor!

Similar to Lisa, Sharon, from Seneca, Missouri, was thrilled to learn of my spiritual research, which affirmed her mother's intuition as well as the experiences of her young autistic children:

Now I know that my two children who just happen to have autism *do* have that special connection with our Lord. There was a time before our son was ever diagnosed, when he was 2 years old, that he pointed to the ceiling and said "man." You can imagine how we felt, but we didn't think much of it until he kept saying that when he was in bed, "I talking to angels." We now know that it wasn't a mistake, but that he was being very honest with us.

Just three days ago, I was bringing Jillian back from a doctor's appointment, and we were driving past a church here in town. She said, "Look mommy! It's Jesus!" I asked where, and she said that He was next to the church. Then I asked what He was doing, and she said "He was praying." I then said, "Does Jesus come and talk to you?" She said yes, so I said that the next time He comes to talk to you, tell Him that mommy loves Him very much, and she said okay. Then she said "He's a nice man!"

By reading Sharon's anecdote, you may be thinking that Jillian's experience could be typical of *any* child with an active imagination; but let's remember that a hallmark of those of us with autism is the very literal interpretation of what is perceived. That is, we tell it like it is because there's no other way to tell it—remember, we say what we mean, and mean what we say. (It's also why we might become distraught upon learning someone has eaten crow, lost their head, or had their heart broken.) Nor does Jillian spontaneously tell of Jesus to gain reward or parental gratification. On the contrary, in his research Dr. Sparrow contends "...most Christ encounters have Jesus speaking to individuals *about his love for them*. Such interventions seem to inspire spiritual work without conferring political or moral advantage upon the recipient." Intriguing, too, is that in several instances, the Jesus stories I received were from families *without* strong religious backgrounds, similar to that of Paula from Peoria, Illinois, mom to son Sean:

My son is very fascinated with Jesus, and a big believer. I finally bought him a Bible, and he has been on me to watch the movie *The Passion of the Christ.* I thought it would be hard for him to watch, but it was not. It was hard for the other siblings, who all cried like I did when I watched it. My oldest asked Sean why it did not make him cry, and he responded by saying, "Jesus had to die on the cross." I later asked him more of his feelings, and he basically summed it up that going to Heaven for eternity is our purpose in life, as it was for Jesus, and that is something to rejoice about, not fear or be sad about.

Dr. Sparrow goes on to explain that pedestrian individuals, even those challenged to integrate with their way of being in the world, are every bit as likely to receive profound visions as those religiously immersed. "One might think that such experiences would come to a very few devout individuals. But from what I have discovered in my preliminary research, Christ encounters apparently happen as much to ordinary individuals who are simply striving in their own way to do their best." Indeed, the essence of Jesus' compassion for a child compromised—at risk of being "less than perfect"—seems evident in this next story from Rose in Corning, Arkansas:

> My son is 9 years old and he is autistic. My son's name is John. He was born three months premature. I had thyroid cancer at the time; we did not know I was pregnant, neither did the doctors. Anyway, I went through a lot of testing for cancer and surgery, and was two months pregnant at the time. There were complications and John was born early.
>
> When we brought him home, my husband would hold him up to the window. It looked like John was looking at someone and we could not see them, but John could. Later, when he was a couple of months old, I had this music box that played a religious song and John would curl up his hands like he was in pain, and point to the palms of his

hands. Also, when he was 3 years old, John said "Jesus" while we were eating. He did not talk much at the time, but he did say "Jesus." If it was not for the Lord, my son would not be here today. The doctors said they did not think he would live because he was in such bad shape, but he survived—the spark of life was in him at the beginning, and it did not go out.

Cheryl from Park City, Utah, told of the miraculous occurrence resulting from her sons' unyielding faith in Christ. Her anecdote exemplifies Dr. Sparrow's observation that oftentimes Christ encounters "almost always seem to represent a pivotal moment in a person's life…"

My 9-year-old son, Grant, has autism, and my 7-year-old son, David, is now [diagnosed] off the spectrum. On October 28, 2002, we had our home enthroned with the Sacred Heart of Jesus on my oldest son Grant's birthday, which is also the feast day of St. Jude, the patron saint of lost causes. Enthronement is a non-essential Catholic tradition. That evening, my children insisted on sleeping in front of Jesus. During this time, the boys were learning about butterflies at school; in light of sensory integration therapies with real world application, I made cocoons for each of them to wriggle in as caterpillars. I told them they would fly like butterflies in the morning. Little did I know a fascinating awakening in my children would take place in the form of attending. Each night the children insisted on sleeping in front of Jesus. This went on for weeks. I finally said we have to sleep in our own beds. They insisted,

"Mommy, no! You need to sleep down here so you can see what happens." I was inspired by the children's attraction, insistence, and passion. Exhausted, I lay down with the light on to appease them, and dozed off into light sleep with the intention of getting up as soon as they were asleep to get into my own bed. I awoke a few minutes later to a host of rainbow-colored, multi-sized clear balls floating above the altar of the Sacred Heart of Jesus. I was completely cognizant...speechless...could not speak if I wanted to...and feeling tranquil and a sadness in my heart, wondering why they had to leave when they were floating away up through the ceiling. Grant said, "The balls remind me of Christmas." He also said they were angels. I have never experienced this since, but never balk when my children want to sleep in front of Jesus.

"Emily is the beat of my heart, she reminds me each day of all of the miracles God performs around us all of the time. Every time she meets a new milestone it gives me and her reason to celebrate this wonderful life God has given us. I can see all of the purpose in her life!" So affirms Kim of her 10-year-old daughter Emily, who is diagnosed with autism, mental retardation, and a "sound-system disorder." But her litany of labels aside, Emily also shares a natural aptitude for accessing Jesus, an aptitude that, for some, might be obscured and overlooked by her diagnoses. From her Warrenton, Missouri, home, Kim writes:

My daughter Emily has a very special personal relationship with Jesus. She will tell you that He is her best friend. We are Christians, and when the spirit of God is strong in a worship service, Emily will start to cry and is overcome with emotion. A few years ago, we went to the store and she stood there and looked at this picture of Jesus; she cried because she wanted it, had to have it. She knew the picture was of Jesus—how, I don't know. Even though we go to church and read the Bible at home, we do not have a picture of Jesus, never did; nor is there one at church. And since she stays with me and does not go to Sunday school, she could not have seen one there.

We went Christmas shopping and went into this store that sells all Christmas things. They had a giant nativity, and Emily knelt on the ground in front of it praying the whole time; we were in the store at least 30 minutes. She loves to lay her hands on people and pray for them. Yes, she knows Jesus and has a very special relationship with Him. Do I think she is an angel? She is my angel, but, no, I don't think she is an angel. What I believe is that because of her innocence, and the purity of her mind, she is able to see things that we don't because we are not so open to them.

Paying attention to things often overlooked is a lesson that I, myself, was caused to appreciate on one occasion several years back, the week before Christmas. As I was driving to the post office, I passed a large, local antique mall and felt drawn to it. I had procrastinated stopping there recently when I felt the same way, but now I resigned to make a brief detour on the way home. As I strolled through three floors of crafts, antiques, and just plain junk, I was left wondering why I was there. On the two occasions that I either audibly spoke or thought, "Okay, show me what I'm supposed to see," I turned a corner and saw an image of Christ. The first was a vintage framed print of Him gathering children about Him during His lifetime; the second was a plaque depicting the crucifixion. I interpreted these synchronicities as simple and comforting "alignments."

I had walked every inch of the place and was checking out, having purchased an old book, but nothing stunningly dramatic transpired. I thought perhaps I was supposed to stumble upon some artifact of mystical relevance or bump into someone that I knew, but nothing.

As I was leaving the store, an older couple walked in with their son, a man with Down syndrome. As we approached one another, the son stopped, looked at me, and gave me his greetings, to which I smiled broadly and said, "Good morning" in return. Looking up, I noticed a sign on the wall behind him remindful that we remember the "Christ" in Christmas. I was also reminded that we must cherish and validate the small, quiet instances such as these, and not be so intent on seeking something more spectacular than real life itself. In that moment, the peaceful greeting the man and I exchanged was precisely what we each required of the world.

eight

Pathways to Spiritual Wellness

*"The most beautiful experience we can have is
the mysterious—the fundamental emotion
which stands at the cradle of true art and true
science."*

—Albert Einstein

A s an advocate and consultant, I regularly hear from too
many adults and adolescents on the autism spectrum who
are severely depressed or suicidal. In one case, a young man
posted to his MySpace page sequential images of the self-
inflicted incisions he carved into his own flesh. Oftentimes, these
are individuals who feel not only abandoned and betrayed by a
prejudicial society, but abandoned and betrayed by their relationship with God. If ever there was an "autism epidemic," it is
their predicament: the absence of hope for love and acceptance.

Finding our spiritual faith is an individual and unique experience for all. Some of us come to it early in life because of
our faith in a Higher Power, instilled in us since birth. We may
draw upon our faith in arduous times and find solace in knowing it offers us loving affirmation. Others are brought up to

~ 167

practice faith, except enacting traditional rituals likens to re-peating by rote without emotional or spiritual commitment—you do it because you believe you're supposed to. And similar to those individuals who contact me in desperation, some of us bitterly lose sight of our faith altogether. I must admit at one time not so long ago, I fell within this oblique sector.

It's not that I was raised faithless. As a very small child, I was intensely and emotionally sensitive, and wept and grieved regularly. This could be induced by something visual that I found dismal and upsetting, or triggered by a certain piece of music or melancholy lyric—many of those on the autism spectrum have shared these kinds of feelings. And yet at some point, I became virtually detached and malcontent. I attribute this to the scornful abuses I endured while growing up. Maybe I was expecting to be saved or rescued. Isn't this what the Creator in whom I was raised to hold my holiest of beliefs should do for one so persecuted?

Any number of us know of the egregious humiliation that comes from being bullied for our differences. Such was my case. I so loved *The Wizard of Oz* as a young boy, and could usually only connect with other children socially if we engaged in some-thing related to *Oz*. Otherwise, I was a fish out of water. A passion such as *Oz* is considered socially-acceptable for a very young child; problem was, I never outgrew it. And I learned the hard way of stigma's staying power—not only for being very quiet, socially aloof, and lacking in physical agility. When my passion (*not* fixation or obsessive-compulsive disorder) was no longer cool, I paid the price through verbal lacerations, rou-tine physical abuse, and daily taunting in the form of being publicly mocked in front of teachers, students, cafeteria staff, and bus drivers. Nor was I the type to shrug it off and get over it. In addition to severe depression, my continual mind-movie-replays of certain painful events led to (what I know now was) post-traumatic stress disorder.

I was in a gray void with no one to turn to except myself. But instead of seeking resiliency by drawing upon the strength of my Creator, I retaliated by pulling away. I cultivated a dark edge that incurred spiteful, sarcastic commentary directed toward others, probably to deflect attention from myself. I withdrew even further into my shell, if that's possible. Picture growing up across the street from a thriving playground, especially when summertime brought daily day-long activities for all neighborhood children. As the oldest of four boys, some of the other kids didn't even realize my younger brothers *had* an older brother because I was never seen or heard from. I was, for all intents and purposes, an invisible non-entity.

When any one of us find ourselves enduring very trying circumstances, we have two options—two pathways—that lie before us. The first path *appears to be* the path of least resistance. It is the path that allows us to wallow in self-pity and feel entirely justified as "the victim" for behaving badly and treating others poorly. After all, we're just reflecting back what was projected upon us, right?

The second path may take some time to discern depending upon the conviction of one's faith. But it is the one and only true path. It is the path that implores us against succumbance of our circumstances, but instead, to rise above circumstance with grace and humility. It is the path that urges us to unveil, to confront, our life experiences—though flawed and faulty they may be, we lay claim to them, and they are uniquely ours alone. We may draw upon our past to the full-est advantage in order to edify others, to requite proactively contingent upon our personal experience. This is the secret meaning of our lives: bequeathing the truth about ourselves through good works and compassionate service to other hu-man beings.

Finding our faith in this manner is a *process*. It rarely hap-pens quickly, although some do dramatically alter their lives as the result of an epiphany such as a serious accident, drug over-dose, near-death situation, or the unexpected loss of a loved one. For others, it needs the accumulation of many learning experiences until we find our footing on the true path—more facile for some than others, especially those left suppressed, disregarded, or persecuted for daring our permanence. This is a test of our faith. I'm reminded of my friend Carl (and those similar to him) who feels that God has done nothing to help; it wasn't until after I turned 40 that my life began to coalesce.

The impetus for my own personal growth came from self-knowledge and self-reflection. As I gravitated to the autism school of life-knowledge, I befriended a number of individuals—brothers and sisters—who shared similar, sometimes signifi-cantly more aspersing experiences. I found myself welcomed into the fold by them and their families. I received validations for my own life experience in gentle, loving ways. I realized that the abuses I prevailed paled in comparison to the lives of so many others. In particular, I took special notice of the warmth and love that radiated from deep within the eyes of those with-out a voice.

As I found my heart defrosting and opening more fully than it ever had, I became attuned to the ways in which my faith was ascending, responding to the call. Every day, I became attentive to the loving signs and signals that manifested around me. Powerful dreams nourished and coaxed me onward, like the one in which I was standing at a podium in a lecture hall counseling other souls on the virtues of being in a paraplegic body. I found myself paying closer attention to the beauty in all of nature: glorious sunsets and delicate, impossibly-intricate plant life. During one winter, three little bluebirds, such as those right out of the song "Over the Rainbow," gathered on a bush outside my office window. At the height of a blizzard, one of them soared right over my house as I was shoveling the driveway. It was a gift received, hand-delivered to me personally; I learned that bluebirds—especially in winter— were rare for my locale.

The more I relinquished hold over a façade that was not authentic, the more I appreciated life: human differences matter not where love reigns. In his studies on the heart's intelligence, John Chilton Pearce confirms, "Turning to the heart automatically serves the best interests of a situation as a whole, rather than the interests of ourselves alone, and, little by little, this begins to be a real benefit for us."

I'm wondering how many other individuals on the autism spectrum are in a place where their faith is strong and they are seeing clearly the manifest ways in which it is truly reflected back to us every day. For some, it may be harder to see than others, especially when trying to discern it through the muck of self-loathing and melancholy despair. But it is there, I promise. I'm living proof. And so, as long as I have my health and a voice to be heard, I will endeavor to be of good service to others—a strong advocate on behalf of those who cannot advocate for themselves. It is the way by which I can give back in appreciation for all the blessings of my life. My one true path.

Harvesting Our Spiritual Reserve

Cultivating our spirituality is like a spring eternal, traditionally a time of renewal and rebirth. For those of us who live in areas where the seasons change distinctively, this analogy is made all the more apparent in ways that are observed. Tiny green sprouts bud and bloom. The perfumed scent of flowers fills the air about us, punctuated by the whirring of darting dragonflies and yellowjackets. Young animals are born; fledgling robins and rabbits, yearling fawns, and field mice all experience the world fresh and anew. The dormancy of winter sloughs away as farmers' crops—wheat and corn—push their way up through the soil and stretch to greet the warmth of the sun. We are blessed with the ability to absorb these and myriad other sights, sounds, and sensations through the gift of our senses. If we think in pictures and mind-movies, as many autistics do, these visuals seem almost tangible in retaining the vibrant crispness of their colorful hues, tucked away in the vaults of our memory awaiting our command to replay and reexperience them again at will. And yet how many others are as observant as we?

For example, as I take my walk I come upon a stunning vision: a stark and majestic tree whose limbs reach skyward.

Its branches are equally balanced by an even number of mirror-image tendril-like arms on either side, framing a late afternoon full moon cupped in its hollow. I am taken by the tree's humble symmetry—this must be the *symme-tree*, I muse. And I think, does *everyone* truly see the beauty in all that God has offered us through the glory of nature? It is always there, all around us; accessible at all times and at no expense to us. But there are those among us who are so caught up in day-to-day life, putting out "fires," and managing perceived chaos, that they bypass the breathtaking sunset and disregard the lillacs'delicate fragrance. We may interpret how we choose to honor our spirituality in ways that are similar. Is faith something we practice all day, every day, by drinking in and relishing to our fill all that is beautiful around us? Or is faith something we reserve to address but one day a week?

Our spiritual commitment compels that we have faith in that which is *unseen*. But is it? Perhaps that's the difference. Just as that which is glorious in life is always there, all around us, and accessible to us in any moment for the asking, so is our faith—if we choose to see it. Therein lies the challenge to each of us. For those of us who bear many struggles every day, seeing the forest for the trees—literally—may feel like an exercise in sullen futility. How can we be expected to reciprocate an appreciation for all of life and nature when we are toiling strenuously at just *being* instead of *becoming*?

Harvesting our spiritual reserve is like gathering the materials necessary to craft an internal fortress built from a foundation of faith, fortitude, and resiliency of self. The carpentry of construction requires that our tools be able, and that our handiwork be full of grace and reverence, for every moment is a gift. This may seem insurmountable to accept when one feels defeated, hopeless, or suffering so. But when we need our faith most, we can draw upon the stock accumulation of our reserves—in the same way that we have carefully catalogued our inventory of gorgeous, awe-inspiring springtime visuals. Christian author and scholar, C.S. Lewis, wrote of a remarkably similar concept in his *Chronicles of Narnia*, "And the memory of that moment stayed with them always, so that as long as they both lived, if ever they were sad or afraid or angry, the thought of all that glorious goodness, and the feeling that it was still there, quite close...would come back and make them sure, deep down inside, that all was well." Pausing to release our frustrations and anxieties, and submitting to the reenactment of our most prized and revered of recollections is a revelation, in and of itself. When accompanied by favored music in times of meditation, we have a sumptuous, sensory feast. Others may wish to lose themselves in dance, writing, drawing, painting, sculpting—anything that stems of solitary, creative expression. The autistic silence within will speak to us if we can clear our minds and focus.

There are those of us who perpetually prolong the nuances of the most recent offense committed against us, and those who visually rewind the slight that instigated an incensed outburst—as many of us on the autism spectrum are wont to do. Achieving stillness of mind and body in order to tap our inner spirituality calls for self-discipline. Acquiesce your own agenda, just listen and *be*, and you may find yourself delightfully bewildered by the visuals and other sensations that come from this time of quiet contemplation. If we choose to play a mind-movie reflecting the ecstasies of a spring eternal instead of destructive, counter-productive memories, we are, as John Chilton Pearce contends, "recalling an event of love or joy through creative imagination [which] throws out a high-frequency bridge from the prefrontal cortex to the limbic-heart circuit." It was this rationale that I employed to be of service to Vic; it is how the higher-frequencies of love lead to unlimited possibilities.

We also have the capacity to draw upon the spiritual reserve of others when our own ration runs the risk of depletion. This is the way of love. We can silently request that our will is strengthened and empowered by the Higher Authority in which we hold dear our most spiritual faith. We may do this through times of prayer or meditation. Or, because we are all created in God's image, we can also draw upon the will of one another to nourish us with similar sustenance. Oftentimes, we just need someone who "gets" us to be a good listener as we ramble and vent and diffuse ourselves of angst. If we are not in a loving spouse-relationship, we may have others accessible to us who will understand our hunger to be fulfilled and revitalized.

A Divine Byway

In the time that I burgeoned beyond my past and accepted my new incarnation, I wrestled with the novelty of the manifesting emergence. None of it was unsettling or frivolous, but I was anxious, still, for resolution—I was struggling to make sense from the purpose of it all. I wanted to enhance my sensitivity in order to better serve those with autism: if I could communicate without words or become a finely-attuned intuit, I might better benefit those without voices, such as Carl. I sought anyone who'd already endured this evolutionary process and could counsel me as it transpired. Amazingly, *no one* to whom I outreached responded, and my continued attempts to do so led nowhere. I was failing at this point, or so I thought. I didn't think my requests for support were unreasonable, and I certainly wasn't looking for guidance *gratis*.

In hindsight, it was necessary for me to create my *own* divine byway to attain authenticity and harvest the spiritual reserve to which I was entitled. For those readers feeling directionless and in need of a rarefied compass or road map, I offer an alternative route to contemplate. In so doing, I now wish to share the fruits of this protocol with others; you'll likely recognize many autistic attributes present naturally in that which I am about to reveal. If we are presuming of intellect, I don't believe there's anything I propose here that cannot be replicated—in its entirety or piecemeal—with my autistic friends under the loving guidance of a trusted ally, and through time. Hopefully, it will have broader application for others beyond autism's borders.

1. Commit to a Higher Power.

    ❀ Acknowledge your place in the universe.

    ❀ Welcome the Creator into your life throughout everyday.

    ❀ Engage with your Creator by celebrating your unique diversity versus current media emphasis on physical perfection, plastic surgery, and makeovers.

☙ The Creator makes no mistakes. Assess your unique gifts and count your blessings—what can you offer others in order to be of service?

In a dream, I was walking my dog early one evening as the sun began to set. We trod down a familiar, isolated dirt road near our home, and directly toward the red-orange sun. I lifted my face to the sun and felt its wonderful warmth spread over my skin. In that moment, I understood that I had been "recognized" by God for who I was, and what I could contribute. It was, and is, a lasting affirmation, and one that I treasure. I knew that God is within each one of us.

2. Daily Prayer or Meditation

☙ Pray or meditate selflessly (that is, *no* winning lottery numbers!).

☙ Do this daily, if only for 5 or 10 minutes.

☙ This process can also include stating intentions or seeking resolution in dreams.

☙ If you can devote longer periods, try visualization exercises to stretch your consciousness and imagination; *never* dismiss imagination—everything around us originated in someone's imagination, even the chair upon which you are seated.

I awakened shortly after midnight having had an awesome, inspirational, and vivid dream. In it, I was in a space, without discernible walls, with a male mentor who was positioned above me, to my right. My mentor gently urged, coaxed, and cajoled me to expand myself through thoughts, words, music, and motion to create a constantly moving, colorful "fantasy-scape"—all of my own doing—a dynamic morphing of preposterous images. It looked as spontaneous and fast-paced as a scene from Who Framed Roger Rabbit? *Set to the bass-line from the Stone Temple Pilot's song "Even Flow" (don't ask me why), it all became real as I imagined and sang it, with my mentor presiding. Soon, I no longer restrained myself, and, once I abandoned my self-consciousness and got into a rhythm that picked up momentum, anything was possible! I had untapped potential, which my mentor helped me to realize in his patience; he celebrated it with me as I went along. In the end, I was left with the distinct impression that "thought creates form." It was this exhilarating realization to which I awakened.*

3. Random Acts of Kindness

    ❀ Determine to increase your sensitivity toward others as opposed to a perpetuating a "Jerry Springer" mentality of retribution and revenge.

    ❀ Perceive every encounter with another human being as an *opportunity*.

    ❀ How can you be of service to others on a daily basis (listening, courtesy, anonymous kindness) without praise or recognition? This is humility.

❀ Throughout every day, silently bless or pray for the wellness of others you perceive less fortunate than yourself. To honor this, I'll silently request that God lighten the load or brighten the day of someone passing by who seems burdened or overwhelmed. This is one way I practice my spirituality on a daily basis.

I was staying at a Holiday Inn, and came down to breakfast at 6:30 a.m. At that hour, I was the only person in the restaurant. Mary, my waitress, introduced herself, apologizing that coffee wasn't yet made. I assured her orange juice and water was fine. Mary had auburn-dyed hair, twinkling eyes, and a docile demeanor. I later learned she was a very young-looking age 75, and still going strong.

As I watched Mary bustle about, I received a brief, empathic "impression." The impression was that she had lost a child, a son. However, I certainly was not about to suggest something so wildly inappropriate to a total stranger. But Mary was gracious and chatty, so, instead, I asked, "Tell me about your family." (As a person with Asperger's, let it be known that it is highly unusual for me to attempt small talk, especially with strangers.)

Mary proceeded to tell me about her 50-year-old son, a successful pilot, who was married to a woman that treated Mary unkindly. She joked that her daughter-in-law needed to "come back" nicer in her next life. She then told me of her 44-year-old daughter, a businesswoman, with two teenage sons. As I listened, I was silently relieved I hadn't risked acting upon my impression. But just then, Mary said, "And I had another son, Dana. He died when he was nine, 25 years ago." As you might imagine, I felt a flood of emotions when she revealed this. But there was more. She added, "He had Down syndrome."

With misting eyes, this gentle woman, who was unknown to me but a few moments sooner, began to divulge thoughts and feelings and memories long dormant. She never got the opportunity to speak of Dana. She had always been made to feel ashamed, "dirty" she whispered. Mary's husband insisted that Dana was a "mistake," all her fault. He never accepted Dana and compelled her to place him with a foster mother. Her husband didn't even attend the funeral. It drove them apart. Although still married, they have lived separately ever since.

When Mary paused, I quietly asked what she had learned from Dana. She replied, "Love and patience." We engaged in a conversation about the prevalence of people with Down syndrome and autism, present in our lives as our teachers. I affirmed that each individual is beautifully and naturally designed just perfectly. She concluded that Dana must've been an angel.

What were the chances that Mary and I—two strangers—would meet and have such a conversation? In reply to my simple "small talk" inquiry about family, she somehow saw fit to count a child long since passed—and qualify his unique difference. Her liberated memories led to a lovely validation for us both, and a special privilege for me, as the recipient.

4. Holistic Health

   ◉ Assess your lifestyle including diet, rest, exercise,
   vocation, and relationships.

   ◉ Endeavor to clear your life of elements that can
   deaden or "block" you, like personal or external
   pessimism, unhealthy diet, drugs, nicotine, alcohol,
   pornography.

   ◉ Determine how you *do* deal with stress and
   negativity—can you view it objectively as an
   outsider looking in, as a learning experience?

   ◉ Examine what you "put out there" in terms of how
   you interact with others (grace, humility, and
   harmless forms of humor versus gossip, lying, and
   duplicity).

   *I've learned to manipulate my nightmares to quell any
   truly frightening elements. Now they are merely annoyances
   if they even occur at all. For me, it's like visiting a movie set,
   watching the action play out before me. I'm merely an
   observer, not an active participant.*

   *Though I hadn't had any traumatizing dreams in years,
   in early December 1998, I had a parting nightmare that
   was as overwhelming in its sensation as the most vivid of
   my dreams. My impression was that it was a vision of hell.
   What I saw, mercifully at a distance, was a large, stainless-
   steel butcher's shop filled with red, raw, disembodied
   human limbs that were still very much alive, writhing and
   quivering with agony. A small, hooded and cloaked*

figure—a character of dwarf-like stature—was directing the heinous machinery. Included was a conveyor belt contraption from which decapitated heads were suspended on hooks. As they neared a rotating drill, each head turned with its mouth open to receive the drill with horrific results that I will leave to your imagination. I awoke in the middle of the night feeling physically ill and nauseated—the first time I had ever been so affected by a nightmare.

The dream had a purpose. I suspect it was to desensitize me in preparation for wherever my future might lead me. Such experiences will make me stronger in enduring real time horrors: I'm aware of pornography in its darkest incarnations, I've committed to memory images in documentaries about Hitler's atrocities, and I've heard the rationales of serial killers. A young man with Asperger's shared a similar logic. He was fascinated with medieval devices of torture, not because he was interested in their grisly effects, but his goal was to be a Christian missionary. He wanted to learn all he could about the devices to prepare for being so persecuted in third-world countries, where those devices are still employed. For him, knowledge is power.

Purging negativity, and either banishing it, or translating it into an artful device, diffuses it of any power or hold over us.

5. Reverence for Nature
   ❂ Every new day is a gift—none of us is guaranteed another—so offer up your heartfelt gratitude.

- Be grateful for inclement weather so that we have balance in order to better appreciate beautiful days.
- Allow fresh air to fill your lungs, and relish it—it's a gift.
- Every day, connect with the sky, stars, trees, flowers, plants, gardens, and all living creatures—you'll get back all the good things you send out.

One night, I had a dream in which my friend Doris was with me in a New York antique and junk shop. We were browsing about, and Doris took a little wrapped mint from a dish set out by the cash register. I took about five of them, unwrapped one, and ate it. Outside the storefront window, a group of rather disheveled, low- or no-income elderly folks had gathered at what seemed to be a bus stop. One woman came in and asked for a mint. The shop owner said they're for sale only, even though he must've known we took some for nothing. I then took care to conceal my others. But after the woman left, Doris asked the owner how much they were so she could buy one. As I watched, she took a mint out, gave it to the woman, and struck up a conversation with her and some of the others. It wasn't like me not to do something similar, but in order for me to have done so I would've had to reveal my pocketful of mints. I was ashamed of myself for not thinking to do what Doris did.

When I awoke immediately following the dream, I felt confused and embarrassed. What was the message in the dream? I put my dog outside, and looked up to see a shooting star in a night sky filled with every conceivable constellation.

I thought, "Wow, how neat and unusual. How many others could've been witness to that just now? Probably no one." Then I thought, "God, if that was you, do it again." But after scanning the sky for a few moments, nothing happened. As I was coming back inside the house, the message of the dream and what just occurred outside coincided with one another in a clarity that now made sense. What hit me foremost was "Don't get greedy and ask for more than what you're entitled to." Second, "Don't be so passive and afraid to take risks at your own expense. Stay focused on what's truly important and do the right thing." Wise lessons to carry with me, and keep me grounded. I silently thanked God.

A little more than 24 hours later, while coming out of the post office, I saw a rather unkempt-looking elderly woman spill more than half a dozen letters all over the floor. As she stooped to reach them, I quickly intervened and gathered them up, feeling that I'd redeemed myself for not behaving similarly in my dream.

6. Visualize Prosperity

   ❀ Reconcile past transgressions against others—can you be forgiving?—and then validate ways you've benefited others, to temper it.

   ❀ Determine and prepare to move forward in order to be of service to others.

   ❀ Pray or meditate for prosperity—not wealth—to be fairly compensated for your good works (this may not come in monetary remuneration).

❂ Visualize where you'd like to be, and what you'd like to be doing in order to serve others—pray and meditate for guidance.

In early October 2002, I was invited to speak about Asperger's Syndrome on campus at an Ohio university. It was an exhilarating experience presenting to more than 250 people of varied backgrounds, and the first time I had ever been applauded going into a break and returning from a break. I also received a standing ovation at the day's end! But better than that, the perpetuity of the message demonstrated itself through a ripple effect in short order.

Immediately after the presentation (and before a question-and-answer reception that evening), two young people who had been in the audience gently approached me. Each had been validated by my words and wanted to connect with me. Barbara is a physically beautiful young woman, 30 years of age, who had a long history of being mislabeled as "learning disabled." She now understood that Asperger's made sense for her. Patrick is a gifted college student also with Asperger's, who almost didn't come that day. The three of us had a wonderful conversation and Patrick and Barbara—previously unknown to one another—realized they lived very near one another, had a lot in common, and developed camaraderie. I invited them both to join me at the reception, which they did.

It was there that Patrick's true greatness really shone through. He was a strong self-advocate, and counseled a mother and father in the room who had a son his age. The parents were really struggling with their son's depression and seeming lack of motivation in life. Patrick offered his insights and provided his contact information as a resource. I publicly acknowledged how extremely proud I was of his beautiful, courageous work. Shortly afterward, he e-mailed to say that he was now inspired to teach others about Asperger's Syndrome and looked to me for course suggestions. I was also able to facilitate his connection with my host, Chris, at the university's student programs office, so that Patrick could be a resource to them in counseling incoming students with Asperger's.

I later received an e-mail from a woman who had been in the audience and who, after a tortuous life, had recently been diagnosed with Asperger's Syndrome. She, too, was now inspired to outreach to others, but because she was distanced from the university, I suggested she contact a similar program in the college closest to her.

A doctor who is the director of behavioral science in the family practice residency program of the local medical center also wrote to thank me for the seminar. Here, too, was another remarkable ripple. This was a person who not only oversaw a program for persons with "behaviors," she also had influence in perpetuating the message as a supervisor for young interns.

Finally, my host Chris and I had maintained contact before, during, and after the seminar. Chris works on campus supporting students with different ways of being, including Asperger's. She is a stunningly young-looking woman in her early 50s with crystal-blue eyes, strong, fine features, and silver hair. She wears flowing dresses and appeared to me as someone with great spiritual tranquility, and I told her so. Her surprising admission was that she didn't consider herself to be a very spiritual person. In my follow-up I risked contradicting her:

> I've been struggling a bit with a comment you made in an e-mail last week about not considering yourself to be a spiritual person. I see in you the exact opposite. You are possessed of a purity and a clarity in your countenance, and a calm and reserve in your demeanor that speaks to such beauty and wisdom. Please think on this.

Chris wrote back to say that my email was the best thing to happen to her all day. In summation of this turn of events, I felt like the richest man in the world.

7. Acknowledge Your Spiritual Guardians, Mentors, and Protectors.

    - Offer praise and gratitude for the protection and learning experiences you've received.
    - Acknowledge those times a Higher Power intervened in your life.
    - Recognize that communications can be symbolic and impressed in dreams or through creative inspiration.
    - Personalize your Guardians, Mentors, and Protectors.

One January Sunday morning, I was thinking fondly of Evelyn, an elderly and dear friend of mine. We had exchanged Christmas greetings, and I wondered when I'd hear from her next. A short while later that morning, the phone rang. It was a wrong number, but the caller asked for "Evelyn." My Evelyn was the only Evelyn I knew. When I told the caller she had the wrong number, her voice so impressed me for its unusual warmth. She apologetically, caringly said, "Oh, I'm so very sorry." It stayed with me. By early evening, Evelyn's daughter called to tell me Evelyn had passed the previous Friday.

While I missed Evelyn, I had no regrets about our relationship. At every opportunity, I wrote or personally told her how very special she was to me. The lesson learned was that the gift is sacred. It is available to the perceiver only when borne of love, compassion for others, and a true desire to perpetuate God's greater good—not for trivial purposes like playing idle guessing games.

Actualization

Whether you are autistic or neuro-typical, being attentive to the ways in which you receive intuitive information—as it relates to our senses—will aid in determining your spiritual gifts, singly or in combination. If by pursuing the divine byway I sent forth, or via other blessed means, you comprehend visions paired with a fleeting scent, this will alert you to perceive future experiences using these senses. Perhaps you have an inner knowing when someone needs the healing comfort of touch.

Or maybe you hear a cryptic calling in your heart on which you are compelled to act. Symbolic information may require deciphering, similar to my exiled bluebirds.

A fitting example of this divine byway in operation is the time I found myself working in Delaware. I was scheduled to conduct a number of environmental assessments. This meant that I would go out into the community to visit group homes for adults with autism and walk every inch of the houses (without them present), barefoot, in order to provide recommendations for the caregivers about adaptations or accommodations they could make to create a more comfortable living environment for their clients. For example, if I turned on a light that was too bright for my eyes, I'd suggest that they try lower wattage or frosted bulbs.

That morning, I prayed to be of good use to the people for whom I would be serving—the individuals with autism. During my prayer, I received a visual impression of a divining rod, vibrating as it was used to locate water underground. I understood it as an analogy for myself. And while riding as a passenger en route to the first location, I thought to myself, "If I'm really supposed to be doing this, show me a *Wizard of Oz* sign." Turning down the rural road on which the first house was located, we passed a farm market with a large scarecrow on its sign, his arms outstretched as if awaiting Dorothy's rescue.

During my walk through each of the four homes I visited, I not only picked up on the environmental subtleties that could be improved upon, but I found myself receiving impressions specific to the people who lived there. Not to be influenced, I was clear in telling those who greeted us in each residence that I only desired to know the number of individuals living there and their sex—nothing more. I don't know how I knew to say what I did, but when it came, it came hard and fast and with authority.

In the first house, I walked into the dining room and sat down. I began rocking in my seat and said, "There's someone in this house that sits and does this here." The house supervisor confirmed that was true; of the five ladies in the house, one preferred to eat alone in that room, and rocked in her chair. Upstairs, I was told that two of the women, who had adjoining rooms, were experiencing great difficulty sleeping at night. As I looked out the second floor window, I saw a horse farm across the field. I said, "I need you to find out what's going on with the horses." My sense was that there was some undetected angst, perhaps being exchanged between the women and the animals, that was heightening everyone's anxiety. The house supervisor replied, "It's funny you should say that because I recently saw the horses rearing and bucking," which was unusual for them. Coming back downstairs, I felt drawn to the living room area and correctly stated that it was a favored area in which all the women felt comfortable.

Walking through the next house, I "knew" that one man had picked out the very specific color blue for his room walls. When told that another man was believed to be experiencing physical pain, I knew that he was about 23 years old (he was), and that he hit his face in a certain place near one eye. I was told that any medical issue, such as migraines or allergies, had been ruled out, but I asked that his eyes be examined. In someone else's room, the house supervisor informed me that one particular man rips his clothes and sheets when very agitated. As she said that, I replied, "He also rips paper." She said, "No, he doesn't," but I repeated, "No, he rips paper, too." In that moment, I opened his cupboard—it was full of ripped and crumpled paper.

At lunch, my escorts and I walked into a Chinese restaurant. I thought of the horses from that morning and immediately saw a large, etched glass panel of two horses in the entrance. By this point, my hands were vibrating, just like the divining rod in my dream.

Arriving at the third home, I knew that the youngest man was age 21, and that he lived in the smallest upstairs bedroom. I also surmised that he was challenging to support because of his communication obstacles, physical pain, and mental health issues.

The fourth house felt very calming with large trees surrounding it. I sensed that a patio was a favored area for two of the four men. Entering one man's room, I turned and said, "This guy isn't autistic." The house supervisor confirmed that, indeed, he was considered severely autistic. I said, "Then there's something *bigger* than autism going on for him." I was told the man grapples with an extreme seizure disorder that can escalate his behavior before and after, and hospitalize him due to its severity. Finally, while debriefing the house supervisor, he observed that in one bedroom I deliberately felt the carpet with my bare feet and, in another room, I lay in bed—an imitation of both men who resided there.

Afterward, I received a validating message from Alisha, one of my escorts. She wrote, "I thank you for allowing us to accompany you and witness your gift. If ever you are in doubt, you are one of God's gifts who walk among us. Thank you for being you." It was a glorious experience; lest you think my tale is too idealistic or beyond your reach, please recall my humble beginnings.

Does my propensity equate with superiority? Absolutely not. I am undisciplined in my humanity, I stumble and relapse. But despite my most fallible frailties, I strive for what is right and true and good and kind. You, too, are poised to become an agent of transformation, and—autism or not—there's no reason why we can't all unite in this endeavor.

nine

The Human Masquerade

*"Beware so long as you live, of judging people
by appearances."*

—Jean de La Fontaine

I honestly think that our son knows more about God,
Jesus, and all things Heavenly than most people will ever
know. But because he can't talk, we are having trouble
getting our church to agree to let him attend Parish
School of Religion (they are classes offered by Catholic
churches for children enrolled in public school to learn
about the Catholic religion, God, Jesus, and so on) or
make his sacraments unless he can demonstrate a "clear
understanding of the sacraments he wants to receive."
So, unfortunately, when I try to go to church now, I do
not feel God's presence. But when I look at my little boy's
face, I not only feel God's presence, but I think I actually
see it.

Not unlike Matthew Moran, the Arizona boy denied
Communion, Suzanne, a Macedonia, Ohio, mother,
writes of a spiritual conflict between the restrictions of her

organized religion and the religion she receives upon beholding Austin, her 5-year-old son with autism. Suzanne's senti-
ments of exclusion are shared by other parents also
sanctioned or unwelcomed in their place of worship. But
when church inclusion works, it works wonderfully as evidenced by Tricia, from Carlisle, Pennsylvania, telling of her
6-year-old son Kyle's involvement:

> Kyle's experiences at church have been huge. With
> the help of his support staff or a church buddy, he is
> successfully attending Sunday School and participating
> in class activities, not just roaming the room touching
> everything. He reads well, so he will help the teacher
> read the lesson each week. His support staff will take
> him walking whenever he needs a break. Kyle sang with
> the children's choir one Easter, amazing me because I
> never thought that he would tolerate the setting, much
> less sing loud and clear above the other kids. Kyle also
> helped me collect the offering one Sunday that we set
> aside to teach that even people with disabilities (as those
> without disabilities call it) have something to offer and
> are one of God's children. He's always eager to attend
> church and its activities. Kyle has taught me many things
> about God even without the words to tell me.

As we've been discovering, there is spiritual purpose for
people with differences being in the world when we renounce
archaic illusions. Unlimited possibilities await us. But chancing the dance of reciprocity requires that we yield our Good
Samaritan fawning, suppress any trace of pious pity, and

humble ourselves as *peers* instead of merciful martyrs tending to the "afflicted" from afar. This attitude makes the difference between the example of Kyle's inclusion and instances of exclusionary practice such as when Kathy, of Rochester, New York, was informed that her church didn't have the "facilities" to involve her young son in catechism classes—for one hour, one day a week. (One resource to engage places of worship in respectfully understanding autism may be found at *www.thethoughtfulchristian.com.*)

We must be ever mindful of the tendency to revert to a culture of fear. Great strides and significant advances are pending our ability to conjoin through meaningful exchanges— to learn and understand one another through many modes of communication. Recollect Barb Rentenbach's invitation to call a truce and meet her in solitude on the autistic glacier. When will we reach the epoch at which point we finally abate to the momentous shift occurring within our grasp? It's not just coming, it is here! Will we embrace it with reverence, or decline into reluctant submission until further and inevitable wake-up calls us to action?

As the first decade of the new millenium draws to a close, confirmation of the tenet *presume intellect* has begun to prevail through emerging research. Meredyth Goldberg Edelson, a clinical child psychologist, discovered generations of literature, dating to 1937, that linked autism with mental retardation— necessitating the retesting of nearly 300 of her own subjects— were based on flawed assertions or contained no empirical research at all. Dr. Goldberg Edelson's administration of non-verbal intelligence examinations heralds a triumph for autistics.

Researchers from Canada and the United Kingdom have since come forth to also dispell antiquated stereotypes about traditional I.Q. scores versus unconventional intellectual capabilities. Yesteryear is the history of denial, a season dimly waning before a dawn of atonement. These recent discoveries do more than cause us to look beyond labels. In concert with our autistic allies, an entrained collaboration—a partnership of hearts and minds in unison—lies before us in a new brotherhood that holds untold promise for all of humanity.

Paul is a grandfather and retired Lutheran pastor from Jenison, Michigan. For him, aspects of this growing cognizance shine through his grandsons' spiritual giftedness—a giftedness with divine origins, and one that, if properly channeled, foretells the untold promise of which I speak:

> The inclusion specialist at school tested Nathan last year and discovered his math skills; then this year, she tested Noah and finds that he has the same math skills. However when she completed the testing for the math skills and savant syndrome, she asked him, "Who is my sister-in-law?" and he wrote her name on his device. Then she asked, "When did she get married?" and he wrote the date on his device. Next she asked "Whose birthday is today?" and he wrote the name. Then she asked, "How do you know?" and he wrote, "God tells me." She asked him next, "Does He tell you everything?" and Noah wrote, "Yes."

Shades of Michael's explanation for accessing God by way of existing as a whole soul in a broken body, Noah's glorious aptitude is but a miniscule glimmer of the untapped potential for the thousands who live in silence, oppression, and misunderstanding. If you only ever saw yourself reflected in a funhouse mirror, you'd accept your distorted image as reality, never seeing yourself with the clarity of others; thus it is remorseful that an otherwise arrogance may cloud our acuity so, for further exquisite examples persist in spilling forth, telling of autism and a God connection. From Arkansas City, Kansas, Janice writes of her son Chris's persistent radiance despite the dire predictions of professionals:

> I am the mother of a non-verbal 14-year-old son with autism. About three or four years ago, we had a missionary from South America visiting our church for a Wednesday evening service. He was not "preaching," but was just telling us about the country he worked in, and the work he did. All of a sudden, he stopped and gave a message in tongues. My son, sitting beside me, repeated word for word—in the same language and as plain as originally spoken—the message that had been given. It seemed to be some sort of Native American dialect; there was no further interpretation, but everyone there was stunned.
>
> There were two more spiritual incidents with Chris within about a six-month period. The one time, a lady gave another message in tongues; again, no interpretation, but my son who had been laying in the pew beside me, came to a sitting position, raised his hands, and smiled, his face absolutely glowing. Again, this message sounded to be in a Native American dialect. The third occurrence involved this same lady; she was sitting on the last pew— Chris and I were very near the front—and the two of

198 ~ The Soul of Autism

them were "singing in the Spirit" to each other, again in Native American dialect. At the time, we lived in Texas, and were attending a small country Assembly of God church.

Chris was originally our foster child; we got him at 3 months of age. His original diagnosis was deaf/blind, severe Cerebral Palsy, and severe mental retardation—probably to be never more than a "vegetable." The doctor said that Chris didn't have any optical nerves at all, therefore there was no hope; and when I reported to him that I felt Chris was seeing, he was very angry with me, and more or less told me I didn't know what I was talking about. He refused to spend more than 10 seconds shining a light in his eyes. He said Chris was blind, and that was that. Chris's teacher learned of a program at the University of Houston College of Optometry especially for special needs children, and it was determined that Chris did have vision. In fact, it was so good, he no longer qualified for vision services.

Chris began sitting alone, crawling on his hands and knees, and pulling up when he was 32 months old—all within a week's time. He is still diagnosed as mentally retarded, but most professionals feel that if he were verbal, that might change. He was diagnosed with autism when he was age 6. At age 7, he began walking, a year after my husband died. All progress has been because of God—we've received very little support or help from the medical profession—and I do not think that He is through with Chris yet.

Such mounting evidence for a holy propensity in some autistics can no longer be ignored. From Ohio comes Debbi's anecdote about daughter Elizabeth's radiant gift for communion with the Creator; similar to Paul's grandson Noah, Elizabeth is the keeper of wisdom untold:

> A few years ago, I had a friend, Tara, who had several miscarriages. The second was especially devastating as she had been about six months along; she lost her second baby in April. I told Elizabeth, who was very upset about it. The next day she said to me, "Tell Tara and Mike God told me they need to try to get their baby in October, and everything will be alright." What makes this statement amazing are two things: the complexity of the sentence, which is beyond her usual communications, and, second, she does not really know the months of the year except May (her birthday) and December (Christmas).
>
> So, I relayed this information to my friend. Their baby was conceived in October. She had a difficult pregnancy; at times it looked questionable whether she would carry this baby to term. Elizabeth prayed unfailingly every night for this baby. She even woke up in the middle of the night one night, realized she didn't pray for her, and said the prayer in the middle of the night. As problems developed, Elizabeth was firm in her conviction, "This baby will be fine...God told me." The following July, they delivered a beautiful, healthy baby girl, much to the joy of Tara and Mike. When I told Elizabeth about the birth, she stated quite calmly, "I know, God told me." To this day, they credit Elizabeth for their healthy little girl.

Not only are some with autism able to utilize their gifts in some semblance of a sacred office, others glimpse the Heavenly realm from which our very humanity emanates. In his vision, Marie's son, of McLean, Virginia, disclosed not only a God-like "king," but also a cosmic power-struggle between good and evil:

> I thought I was the only one who may believe that my son can talk to angels. About two months ago, my son told me that the angels had come to visit him when he was a baby. He said he was scared at first, but they told him that he was okay. They sang to him. They told him he would talk. Also, that they loved him.
>
> A few days ago, he told me more about the angels. He said that there is a man who talks to the angels. I asked what his name is, and he said "King," and he lives in a kingdom (just so you know, we don't go to church, and he's never with anyone church-affiliated). He said that the man is his father, and loves him. He said that he will go there someday. I asked where, and he went to the window and pointed up to the moon.
>
> He also said that there is also another bad man, and that he is in battle with the angels. He's very scary, he said.
>
> I've tried to lead him on in the wrong direction, such as whether the angels have guitars, and so on. He said, no, they only sing with their mouths. He says they are about 2-and-a-half feet tall—he showed me this.
>
> It's really weird, but he feels comfort and love from the "angels," and believes that the man, "King," is his father, and loves him as well. The way he talks about it, it's like it's real—not like a TV show or something.

To offer some perspective, from West Frankfort, Illinois, Gail's young son, Neil, tells of the human masquerade—God's grand plan for humankind—and our roles in flesh-and-blood disguise as theatre-in-the-round actors:

My son Neil has been diagnosed as being somewhere on the [autism] spectrum. He is very high-functioning and is 9 years old. I suspect he is probably an Asperger's child, but there are varying opinions. Thankfully, Neil is a great communicator!

We were talking about things before bed, and I asked him if he was an advanced soul; this is a subject that we haven't touched on before. He thought for a moment, and said that advanced souls are summoned by God to come back to earth, and live in these costumes because they have unfinished business. He said it is kind of like skipping a test: if you don't do it, you still have to come back and repeat it. He also indicated that God began as a speck of magic dust, and that He looked around and decided to decorate the universe. Solar systems are like a room in a house to Neil. He says God was lonely, so then He created people.

Neil says God created the big bang that brought about everything. Neil has always had an innate insight into spiritual matters. It is not that I have taught him these ideas. Certainly, as a mother, I have shared certain concepts; but we really haven't gotten into the area of reincarnation. By the way, Neil says that he just knows things. It's a gift from God. For example, we had lost a Scrabble game for about a year. He came to me one day, out of the blue, and told me it was in the very top of my cedar closet. It is a place that I can't even reach without a chair. He can't possibly get up there, or see into it at his height. He told me it was a spiritual message.

Neil is a very positive and happy person. He is charming and witty. Neil is also a cancer survivor, having been off of his chemo treatment for almost a year now. He says he sent his leukemia out into space, and told it to never come back and bother anyone else. I am truly blessed to have him in my life!

Staying the Course

As a Catholic sister and an autistic, Penelope McMullen of New Mexico, is also a practitioner of the spiritual aspects of autism; she, herself, has strongly experienced the God connection. As an adult, her dual background poises her as an insightful intercessor in interpretation of the preceding examples of divine giftedness:

I believe that all people have the potential for psychic skills, but that persons with autism may be more apt to develop extrasensory skills because their sensory processing is so problematic. Examples include Thomas McKean, who talks about feeling other people's emotions, and Donna Williams, who frequently "saw" in her mind what her classmates were doing at home (when she'd ask them at school the next day, she'd find out that her visions were accurate). Donna also once saw the Spirit of someone shortly before he died, and she has dreams that accurately foretell future events.

I, too, have psychic dreams. Once I dreamt the content of a letter the day it was written, two days before I received it. I have had other psychic experiences, also. I usually know when someone I am connected to is dying; I have feeling sensations during the moment when a man-made disaster occurs, such as the Pan-Am bombing, the Challenger explosion, and the Rodney King riots. Sometimes I know who is affected or what is happening, but usually I have to wait for a phone call or the next news hour on the radio or television to find out what specifically happened. Less frequently, I get "flashes" of knowing something. For example, once I watched a man I had never seen walk up my driveway as he came to join the tutoring team I coordinate, and I "heard" in my head "he's all talk and no action." After two months he had not followed through on any tasks given to him, and I knew that my "flash" had been accurate.

One of my counselors, who had traveled around the country helping parents of autistic children, said she had never met an autistic person who wasn't deeply spiritual. Each year, the MAAP (More Advanced Individuals with Autism, Asperger's Syndrome, and Pervasive Developmental Disorder) conferences include a session with a panel of autistic adults speaking about their own spirituality. When I attended this session at the 1996 conference, the speakers testified that it was their spirituality that enabled them to survive their life with autism. Some said that without their faith, they would have considered suicide. One, Phil Wheeler, explained that he talks to God "all the time to figure out stuff."

Another panel speaker said she often gets angry at God. She thought that meant maybe she didn't really have faith. But I believe that even being angry is a way of engaging oneself with God. When I was 11 years old, my mother was horrified when she heard me yell, "Jesus Christ!" She thought I was swearing, but I was actually demanding his attention. I still yell, even scream, at God, and amazingly, in the midst of the scream, I always hear an answer that guides me. There's an Hasidic tale about God waiting for us to demand justice before giving it—maybe we all need to learn to yell at God!

Many consider an appreciation of nature to be an important part of their spirituality. I learned I was not the only autistic child who would go off to the woods or sit by a creek for spiritual healing. As an adult, when I am upset I can still go for a walk in the mountains or sit among flowers in a garden and return home calm and happy. Some of the people in my life have expressed surprise when I prefer to pray outside rather than in a church.

Despite the common misconception that autistic people do not have feelings for other people's situations, there are many recorded instances of their empathy. I believe that feeling compassion (which means "feeling with") or empathy for another person is part of the human spiritual experience, and that the amazing number of autistic adults who desire to help others do so from a spiritual base. Kathy Lissner Grant, for example, believes that "when someone is suffering, Christ is hurting, Christ is there being tortured."

As already mentioned, autistic people are able to expand their concern for people to include global issues. For many of us, working for global peace and economic justice is an essential aspect of our spirituality.

For some, empathy extends to all living creatures. For example, Temple Grandin treats with respect the animals she works with because she believes that they, just as much as people, are part of God's creation. Respecting the animals' feelings has made it possible for her to design equipment that keeps livestock calm.

Earlier, I mentioned the psychic tendencies of people with autism. I consider psychic ability to be part of one's spirituality, because it means the person is connected to another on a level outside the usual physical ways of connecting. When I sense that someone I know is dying, or that some tragedy is taking place, I spend some time in prayer as soon as possible. Once this happened while I was driving, so I just pulled over and parked to pray for 10 minutes before going on.

Learning how autism has affected my life has helped me to put my experiences in perspective. I am more understanding of both myself and others, and I have begun to compensate for some of the sensory, communication, and social difficulties that accompany autism. I have also learned to find the diamonds among the coal.

I believe that my experience of autism has deepened my spirituality, and has made me more aware of God's loving guidance. It has been when I have felt most abandoned by people or frustrated with myself that I have also felt most supported by God, because something seemingly magical always happens to help me through any crisis. I understand the Scripture saying, "it is when I am weak that I am strong" (II Corinthians 12:10), because it is in my weakness that God takes over. Who would ever have thought, for instance, that an autistic person could raise funds to tutor 200 low-income students annually? I do not believe I could have done this without supernatural help.

After many years of confusion and frustration, I have changed from being ashamed of my autistic struggles to being proud of what God has done in me. I now live my life with a quiet joy, knowing that I am profoundly loved by the greatest Lover of all, and all I have to do is accept that Love.

Similar to Penelope McMullen, Karly, from Stillwater, Minnesota, is a lover of God. She is a 21-year-old young woman who is also passionate about music and horses. Karly's form of autism, known as Rett's syndrome, is uncommon and almost solely affects little girls. At an early age—and for reasons unknown—females with Rett's lose many previously acquired skills including motor-coordination, which impedes the ability to walk or care for one's self, and often any verbal ability dissipates, as is true of Karly. Her way of being presents laborious obstacles every day, such as communicating through technology that supplants spoken language. But Karly's compensation—existing in a state of solitude—serves to temper her trying life with universal insight about the fundamental nature of God: His accessibility is without boundaries, His love is not held in exclusive reserve for elitists most devout, as Karly explains:

> Others who are Christians have a very limited view of God. It is hard for them to be open to having others' ways of having a relationship with God. They see through their minds, and not their hearts. It is hard for them to see the truth of my experience, of my walk with God. That's what I'm concerned about. It is too easy for people to judge. I don't want to struggle so much, but God is not ready to have me come home. I will be happy when He calls me home. It will be a wonderful day for me. It will be so freeing. I am not afraid. It is God's choice that I stay longer. The reason I am here is to help others see God in a better way...I am ready to go. I don't like to struggle so much, but it will help others. People have complicated God so much. I wish they knew what I have seen. It would change so many things for this world.

Our flesh is but a temporary vehicle in which to house the soul, and each of us furnishes our respective role in the world contributing so our Creator might "see and experience His Godliness through us," as my friend Michael portends. But do not be deceived; wise and wonderful teachers walk among us in disguise as those who appear severely compromised—society's castoffs by some. Karly's station as an intercessor is manifest, though she expectantly awaits deliverance from the perishment imposed upon her by an intolerant society. In concession, one gentle colleague engenders absolute equality to those who abide as Karly does; for the right to live lives to the fullest, to be treated with respect and dignity, and be acknowledged for their courage. "There are many forms of freedom and many forms of suffering. That is why I say believe in yourself. Trust yourself."

If we are not, as Father Pierre Teilhard once said, human beings having a spiritual experience, but spiritual beings having a human experience, therein lies opportunity for kindred connections regardless of our perceived differences. Within the expansive autism industry, there should be *unlimited possibilities* for listening to the wisdom and expertise of those who live it, allowing autistics to self-determine how their lives will and should be—and fairly compensating them for their wealth of invaluable knowledge. Until we shatter demeaning myths and stereotypes and dismantle walls of indifference, the voices of those with autism will continue to be held at bay and silenced by the very industry that purports to know best.

Collaborating to create authentic change requires that we risk committing acts of pure altruism. At present, there is no single self-advocate who is the Rosa Parks of autism, the one whom others both defame and capitulate. But the sacrifice bestowed upon us by the Karlys of the world offers perspective on our actuality—the mission of the human masquerade—by inviting us to perceive our spirituality through an autistic prism. In so doing, Karly's conclusion petitions us to a catalytic occasion: will we accept her solemn invitation to know what she has seen with requisite reverence, and can we look beyond labels to honor the intent of the heart savant?

Bibliography

"Autistic Children Benefit Greatly from Relationship Development Intervention™ Program." *Medical News Today*, April 20, 2005.

Beckman, Mary. "The Case of Mistaken I.Q." *Science NOW Daily News*, February 20, 2006.

Bello, Marisol. "FBI: Hate Crimes Escalate 8% in 2006." *USA Today*, November 20, 2007.

Bergman, P., and S.K. Escalona. "Unusual Sensitivities in Very Young Children." *The Psychoanalytic Study of the Child*, 3/4:333–352. New York: International Universities Press, 1949.

"Born Believers? UA Researcher Examines Biological Bases for Religious Belief." University of Arkansas press release, February 20, 2006.

Bower, Bruce. "Hidden Smarts: Abstract Thought Trumps IQ Scores in Autism." *Science News*, July 7, 2007; Volume 172, Number 1.

Bowers, Keri. "A Journey to Normal." *The Autism Perspective*, Winter 2006; Volume 2, Issue 1.

Buchholz, Ester. "The Call of Solitude." *Psychology Today*, January/February 1998.

Callahan, Kathy L., PhD. *Unseen Hands & Unknown Hearts: A Miracle of Healing Created Through Prayer*. Virginia Beach: A.R.E. Press, 1995.

Carter, Steven. "Professor Challenges Autism Assumption." *The Oregonian*, November 25, 2006.

Cassata, Donna. "Modern Americans a Rude, Boorish Lot?" The Associated Press, October 14, 2005.

Chopra, Deepak. "Seeing What You Believe, Believing What You See." *Forbes.com*, April 18, 2006.

Clancy, Michael. "Church Denies Communion to Autistic Boy." *The Arizona Republic*, March 4, 2006.

Cornell, Eric. "What was God Thinking? Science Can't Tell." *Time*, November 14, 2005.

Dobbin, Ben. "Autistic Team Manager Makes Hoop Dream Come True." The Associated Press, February 24, 2006.

Dodds, Chris and Alexandra Levit. "Kindred Souls." *The Autism Perspective*, Winter 2006; Volume 2, Issue 1.

Dossey, Larry, MD. "The Return of Prayer." *Alternative Therapies in Health and Medicine* 3(6):10–17, 113–120.

Dunne, Brenda J. "Co-operator Experiments with an REG Device." Princeton Engineering Anomalies Research, Princeton University, December 1991.

Dyer, Wayne. *Inspiration: Your Ultimate Calling*. New York: Hay House, 2006.

"Expensive School of Shock brings Pain but no Educational Gain for San Diego Student with Autism." Closed national listserv, June 27, 2007.Fields-Meyer, Tom. "Finding My Son at the Zoo." *People*, April 23, 2007.

Fitzpatrick, Tony. "Teenager Moves Video Icons Just by Imagination." *Washington University in St. Louis News and Information*, October 9, 2006.

Gage, Toni. "No, Don't Say it Louder." *The Autism Perspective* 2, no. 2 (2006).

Gernsbacher, Morton Ann, PhD. "Toward a Behavior of Reciprocity." August 7, 2006.

Goldberg Edelson, Meredyth. "Are the Majority of Children With Autism Mentally Retarded? A Systematic Evaluation of the Data." Williamette [Salem, Oregon University Web site, n.d.

Gonnerman, Jennifer. "School of Shock." MotherJones.com, August 20, 2007.

Gutierrez, Rosalind and Isabella Rice. "Church Seeks Boy's Full Return to Communion." *The Catholic Sun*, March 16, 2006.

Hammons, Steve. "Navy Dolphins may be Deployed: Did Secret ESP Research Involve Them?" *The American Chronicle*, February 14, 2007.

Harmon, Amy. "How About Not 'Curing' Us, Some Autistics Are Pleading." *The New York Times*, December 20, 2004.

———. "In Their Shoes: Prenatal Test Puts Down Syndrome in Hard Focus." *The New York Times*, May 9, 2007.

Hartmann, Ernest. *Boundaries of the Mind: A New Psychology of Personality*. New York: Harpercollins, 1991.

Haught, Nancy. "Rapture Index Spikes after Year of Disasters." *The Portland Oregonian*, December 25, 2005.

Henderson, Mark. "The Man Who Can Open His Emails by Power of Thought." *Times Online*, July 13, 2006.

Higgins, Michael. "Shock Therapy Called Cruel; Kin Disagree." *The Chicago Tribune*, March 8, 2007.

Highfield, Roger. "How Babies Can Read Minds From Age of One." *Telegraph* (U.K.), June 19, 2006.

Huicochea, Alexis. "Man Lifts Car Off Pinned Cyclist: Teenager Expected to Survive Dragging." *Arizona Daily Star*, July 28, 2006.

Hyson, Michael T., PhD. "Dolphins, Therapy, and Autism." Sirius Institute Puna, Hawaii, November 23, 2003.

Iacobelli, Pete. "Schiavo's Sister Chastises Court Ruling." The Associated Press, January 22, 2006.

Jawer, Michael. "A Neurobiology of Sensitivity? Sentience as the Foundation for Unusual Conscious Perception." *Science & Consciousness Review*, January 17, 2007.

———. "Environmental Sensitivity: Inquiry into a Possible Link with Apparitional Experience." *Journal of the Society for Psychical Research* 70 no. 882 (2006).

Johnson, George. "Testing Faith: Science and Religion, Still Worlds Apart. *The New York Times*, April 9, 2006.

Jozsef, Macy. "Living from the Heart." *The Autism Perspective* 2 no. 2 (2006).

Kantrowitz, Barbara and Julie Scelfo. "What Happens When They Grow Up?" *Newsweek*, November 27, 2006.

King, G.A., L. Zwaigenbaum, S. King, D. Baxter, P. Rosenbaum, and A. Bates. "A Qualitative Investigation of Changes in the Belief Systems of Families of Children with Autism or Down Syndrome." *Child: Health, Care and Development*, May 2006.

Kumar, Seema. "Humans Genes Closer to Dolphins Than any Land Animals." *Discover Channel Online News*, January 1998.

Licauco, Jaime. "Inner Awareness: No Conflict Between Religion and the Paranormal." *Philippine Daily Inquirer*, August 1, 2006.

Lilly, John Cunningham, MD. *Lilly on Dolphins: Humans of the Sea*. Anchor Books, 1975.

Loven, Jennifer. "Bush Pays Visit to 17-Year-Old Autistic Basketball Hero." The Associated Press, March 14, 2006.

McGovern, Cammie. "Autism's Parent Trap." *The New York Times*, June 7, 2006

McMullen, Penelope. "The Gifted Side of Autism." *Focus on Autism and Other Developmental Disabilities* 15, no. 4 (2000).

McPherson, Clair. "Solitude in the Faith Traditions." *Spirituality & Health*, January/February 2006.

Mott, Maryann. "Did Animals Sense Tsunami Was Coming?" *National Geographic News*, January 5, 2005.

Neyfakh, Leon. "Regents Consider Action on School that Uses Shocks." *The New York Sun*, May 25, 2006.

Noe, Denise. "Tim: The Boy Who wasn't Meant to Be." *Vox Populi*, August 22, 2006.

Norton, Amy. "Low-Cost Therapy Shows Promise for Autism." Reuters Health, April 19, 2005.

———. "School Programs for Autistic Kids Found Lacking." Reuters Health, July 13, 2007.

"Paralysed Man's Mind Is 'Read.'" *BBC News*, November 15, 2007.

Pearce, Joseph Chilton. *The Biology of Transcendence: A Blueprint of the Human Spirit*. Rochester, Vermont: Park Street Press, 2002.

"Polish Man Wakes From 19-Year Coma." Reuters, June 2, 2007.

Rials-Seitz, Chris. "A Gifted Autistic: A Candid Interview of Johnny Seitz." *The Autism Perspective*, Spring 2006; Volume 2, Issue 2.

Rentenbach, Barb. "What Are Friends For?" *The Autism Perspective*, Winter 2006; Volume 2, Issue 1.

St. John, Patricia. *The Secret Language of Dolphins*. New York: Summit Books, 1991.

Saletan, William. "The Deity in the Data: What the Latest Prayer Study Tells Us About God." *Slate.com*, April 6, 2006.

Shermer, Michael. "Prayer and Healing: The Verdict is in and the Results are Null." *eSkeptic*, the e-mail newsletter of the Skeptic Society, April 5, 2006.

Smith, Stacy Jenel. "Autism Fact of Daily Life for Celebs Whose Children are Affected." *Netscape.com*, April 20, 2006.

Smith Nessel, Sarah. "'Normal' Shouldn't be Only
    Acceptable Realm." *The Kansas City Star*,
    February 11, 2007.

Sparrow, G. Scott., EdD. *I Am with You Always: True
    Stories of Encounters with Jesus*. Bantam Books, 1995.

"State to Continue Funding Shock Therapy School." CBS
    Radio, Inc., June 19, 2006.

Stillman, William. *Autism and the God Connection:
    Redefining the Autistic Experience Through Extraordinary
    Accounts of Spiritual Giftedness*. Naperville, Ill.:
    Sourcebooks, Inc., 2006.

Taylor, Ginger, M.S. "Requesting Answers and Actions from
    Autism Speaks." *AdventuresinAutism.com*, June 28, 2007.

Teasdale, Wayne. *The Mystic Heart: Discovering a Universal
    Spirituality in the World's Religions*. Novato, California:
    New World Library, 1999.

Wallenchinsky, David. "The World's 10 Worst Dictators."
    Parade, January 22, 2006.

Wallis, Claudia. "Inside the Autistic Mind." *Time*, May 15, 2006.
——. "The Down Dilemma." *Time*, November 21, 2005.

Wheldon, Julie. "Ethical Row Erupts Over Designer Babies
    Breakthrough." *The London Daily Mail*, June 19, 2006.

Willing, Richard. "Violent Crime on the Rise, Summit
    Participants Say." *USA Today*, August 31, 2006.

Wilson, Sarah, and Brian Kilcommons. "See the World as
    Your Pets do." *Parade*, October 15, 2006.

Zheng, Yuxing. "Online Child Porn More Brutal, Group
    Reports." The Associated Press, April 17, 2007.

Index

C

Callahan, Kathy, 81
Cather, Willa, 153
Catholic Sun, The, 22
celebrity behavior, 34
Center for Disease Control and
    Prevention, 35
child sex predators, internet, 34
Children of the New Earth, 10
chip in the brain, 90
Chopra, Deepak, 40-41, 58
Christ-like figures, 154
Chronicals of Narnia, 174
Clark, Dick, 50
Clark, June, 9
communication with benign,
    ethereal entities/angels, 26
communication with trees and
    shrubs, 94-95
Compassionate Alignment, 91-96
conditions, degenerative neuron-
    muscular, 64
confrontation and Vic's story, 141-146
connection with a loved one's
    Spirit, 26
consciousness,
    defining, 19-20
    the dichotomy of, 63-75
cookie-cutter approach, 80
countering the culture of fear, 41-47
Course in Miracles, A, 68-69
course, staying the, 202-208
crime is coming back, 34
Cytogenetics and Cell Genetics, 110

D

Daily Mail, 19
Dallas Zoo, the, 97-98
Day of the Dolphin, 110
delphinidae, the, 108
designer babies, 19
Devil's Rejects, The, 33
*Diagnostic and Statistical
    Manual of Mental Health
    Disorders*, 120
dichotomy of consciousness, the,
    63-75
Disabled People. The British
    Council of, 19
Divine entities, 130
Dodds, Chris, 16
dolphin facts, 111
*Dolphin,
    Day of the*, 110
    Man and, 110
dolphin, the voice of the, 108-116
*Dolphin-Human Interaction
    Effects*, 114
*Dolphins, the Secret Language of
    the*, 108
Donoghue, Dr. John, 90
Dossey, Larry, 81
Down Dilemma, The, 18
Down syndrome, 18, 165
down-identified fetus, aborting a, 18
drift, permitting autistics to, 68
Dyer, Dr. Wayne, 86

E

Earth, Children of the New, 10
Edelson, Meredyth Goldberg, 195
EEG, 84, 114

Einstein, Albert, 167
EKG, 84
electric shock treatment, 43-44
eSkeptic, 80
ESP, 108
ESPN, 20
evolution-versus-intelligent
    design controversy, 20
exercise to experience autism, an,
    64-66

F

Facilitated Communication, 61-62,
    72, 85
families with autism, changes in
    belief systems of, 36
FASTER, 18
FC, 61, 72, 85
feeling privileged to have been
    picked to parent a child with
    autism, 39
Film Festival, Berlin, 17
First and Second Trimester
    Evaluation of Risk, The, 18
Fischer, Nicki, 9
Francis of Assisi, Saint, 101-102
Francis, Linda, 9

G

Golden Books, Little, 128
Good Samaritan, 194
Goodall, Jane, 97
Graduated Electronic Decelerator, 44
Grandin, Temple, 98
grandparents, connections with
    deceased, 125-127

*Guideline for the Celebration of
    the Sacraments with Persons
    with Disabilities*, 21

H

happy slapping as the latest crime
    craze, 34
Harmonious Patterns, 79-96
Hartmann, Earnest, 120
Harvard
    Medical School, 80
    School of Public Health, 46
Health, Holistic, 181-182
HeartMath, Insistute of, 84, 114
Heightened Perceptual Senses, 108
Holiday Inn, 179
Holistic Health, 181-182
Hostel, 33
HPA, 108
human bonds, power in, 81
Human Development, The
    Institute of Health and, 18
Hyperesthesia, 120

I

I Am with You Always, 155
in-Spirit, 86
Institute of Health and Human
    Development, the, 18
intercessory prayer, 81
intercessory, meaning of, 81

J

Jahn, Robert G., 89
Jesus Christ, suggesting the
    second coming of, 27

V

Vibration Regulation Therapy, 92
Visualize Prosperity, 184-187
VRT, 92

W

Washington Post, 18
Weaver, Sigourney, 17
Who Framed Roger Rabbit?, 178

Wisdom and unlimited
    possibilities, 208
Wizard of Oz, The, 46, 79, 168, 189
Wolfcreek, 33
world needs autism, the, 33-62
WTAE-TV, 136

Z

Zagar, Teo, 9
Zukav, Gary, 9

About the Author

WILLIAM STILLMAN is author of the groundbreaking work, *Autism and the God Connection: Redefining the Autistic Experience Through Extraordinary Accounts of Spiritual Giftedness*. His other books include: *The Autism Answer Book, The Everything Parent's Guide to Children with Asperger's Syndrome: Help, Hope and Guidance, The Everything Parent's Guide to Children with Bipolar Disorder: Professional, Reassuring Advice to Help You Understand and Cope*, and *Demystifying the Autistic Experience: A Humanistic Introduction for Parents, Caregivers and Educators*, which has been highly praised by the autism and self-advocacy communities. Stillman also writes a column, "Through the Looking Glass," for the national quarterly publication *The Autism Perspective*, and is a regular contributing writer, and is on the magazine's advisory board. (Stillman is also coauthor of several successful books about his life-long passion, *The Wizard of Oz*.)

Autism and the God Connection, Stillman's study of profound spiritual, mystical, and metaphysical giftedness of some individuals with autism, has resonated with parents, professionals, and persons with autism internationally, and has received endorsements of praise from bestselling authors Gary Zukav, Carol Bowman, Dean Hamer, and Larry Dossey. In 2007, it was nominated as a finalist for Publishers Marketing Association's prestigious Benjamin Franklin Award for excellence. Inspired by *Autism and the God Connection*, Stillman hosts a monthly question-and-answer column for *Children of the New Earth* magazine, and he has developed an autism guide for The Thoughtful Christian, a theological training and resource organization. The film rights to *Autism and the God Connection* have been optioned for a proposed documentary.

As an adult with Asperger's Syndrome, a mild "cousin" of autism, Stillman's message of reverence and respect has touched thousands nationally through his acclaimed autism workshops and private consultations throughout the United States. Stillman has a BS in education from Millersville University in Pennsylvania, and has worked to support people with different ways of being since 1987. He was formerly the Pennsylvania Department of Public Welfare, Office of Mental Retardation's statewide point person for children with intellectual impairment, mental health issues, and autism.

Stillman is founder of the Pennsylvania Autism Self Advocacy Coalition (PASAC), which endeavors to educate and advise state and local government, law enforcement, educators, and the medical community about the autism spectrum from the "inside out." He served on Pennsylvania's Autism Task Force, and is on several autism advisory boards. He is the coordinator for a Pennsylvania-based meeting group of individuals who use Augmentative and Alternative Communication. Stillman has also collaborated with Youth

Advocate Programs' relationship-based autism curriculum, which will set the national standard by which mental health workers will be trained to support children and adolescents with autism and mental health issues.

In his work to support those who love and care for individuals with autism and Asperger's Syndrome, Stillman sets a tone for our collective understanding of the autistic experience in ways that are unprecedented. Autism should not be defined as an "affliction endured by sufferers," but as a truly unique and individual experience to be respected and appreciated by all. In so doing, Stillman highlights the exquisite sensitivities of our most valuable, wise, and loving "teachers."

William Stillman's Website is *www.williamstillman.com*.